Religion, Occult and Youth Conflict in the Niger Delta of Nigeria

Edlyne E. Anugwom

Langaa Research & Publishing CIG
Mankon, Bamenda

Publisher:
Langaa RPCIG
Langaa Research & Publishing Common Initiative Group
P.O. Box 902 Mankon
Bamenda
North West Region
Cameroon
Langaagrp@gmail.com
www.langaa-rpcig.net

Distributed in and outside N. America by African Books Collective
orders@africanbookscollective.com
www.africanbookscollective.com

ISBN-10: 995676499X

ISBN-13: 9789956764990

© Edlyne E. Anugwom 2017

Table of Contents

Acknowledgements

The manuscript of this book was conceived and begun during my three months stint as a fellow at the Netherlands Institute for Advanced Study in the Humanities and Social Sciences (NIAS), Wassenaar (now moved to Amsterdam), the Netherlands in 2009. It benefitted both from the reaction to my presentation on the subject-matter at the customary inaugural fellows' seminar at the center and the comments and suggestions generously offered by other fellows who were intellectually aroused and intrigued within this three month period. In this connection, I wish to thank in particular Johan Heilbron (Centre de Sociologie Europeenne, Paris); Anna-Maria Brandstetter (Johannes Gutenberg University, Mainz); Matthias Henze (Rice University, Houston USA); Cynthia Vialle (Leiden University); Astrid Erll (University of Wuppertal) among others who also provided companionship and advice.

The movement from manuscript to book evidently took a long gestation period and this presented challenges of the indefiniteness and ambivalence of picking-up one's thought from where it was left off after months of engagement in other activities. However, the duration offered ample opportunity for critical introspection and embodiment of new developments in the Niger Delta narrative. I believe the constant rewriting or refinement as it were added value to the book. I also acknowledge the wonderful work done by my research assistants – Achu Vitus Amadi and Kemeaweregha Tebogren.

In addition to the above mentioned individuals, I must express my gratitude to my colleagues in the Department of Anthropology and Sociology at the University of the Western Cape, South Africa especially Professors Oloyede; Gibson and Nadasen who graciously (without knowing it) granted me time away from normal departmental business to tidy-up the manuscript. I equally acknowledge the untiring efforts of my brother and friend, Francis Nyamnjoh (of the University of Cape Town) who has been unwavering in egging me on and supporting me all these years. I must also acknowledge the efforts of my friend, Mwenda Ntarangwi who graciously took time off his busy schedule to write the foreword. Finally, I thank the entire wonderful people at Langaa RPCIG for their usual promptness and efficiency in once more 'publishing Africa in Africa'.

I wholeheartedly acknowledge responsibility for all and any shortfalls in this book.

Edlyne Anugwom
Bellville, 30 October 2016.

Foreword

Studies abound of youth around the world intervening on behalf of their communities for social justice. Among these studies are emerging concerns of how youth, feeling disempowered and marginalized, seek alternative forms of power to influence their desired outcomes. This phenomenon is highly visible in Africa where struggles to access limited public resources go hand in hand with social expectations for youth to wait their turn to lead. In Nigeria there are two factors that converge to make the role of youth even more critical. The oil boom of the 1970s produced a certain sense of security that saw the government engage in extravagant spending or what some may consider conspicuous consumption. Then there was misrule perpetuated by a series of military dictatorships and corrupt regimes that almost became institutionalized. As citizens tried to navigate everyday life amid these two competing strategies, the country became even more stratified with the rich getting richer and the poor poorer. Certain regions such as the Niger Delta with its rich oil fields became spaces for prolonged fighting for resources. The wealth of the region was not evenly distributed. Having oil of gold in one's region did not translate into access to its monetary value. Poverty continued to have a strong hold on the people even as a few well-connected individuals extracted the natural resources and made fortunes from it. During Abacha's regime, for instance, the Niger Delta became militarized, local community members revolted against the state for annexing local resources, and the government responded with heavy-handed military repression. This military response emboldened youth in the community to seek ways of fighting back. This relationship continues to shape much of their response to resource management in the area today. As Edlyne Anugwom shows in this volume, Niger Delta youth especially in Ijaw, are at the forefront of seeking socioeconomic justice on behalf of their community. Throughout Africa indigenous communities find themselves caught up in the contentious reality of sitting on resources that they cannot exploit for their benefits. How is

ix

it that the regions supplying most of the resources end up not benefiting from them? Anugwon explains thus, "popular discourse in the Niger Delta [is] that the wealth from the region has been taken to transform an almost arid land space in Northern Nigeria [Abuja] into a paradise while the region from which the wealth is gotten has been left desolate." This disparity, often observed as community members from the Niger Delta visit Abuja and other cities motivates the youth to seek redress of a long-term, state-sanctioned economic marginalization and exploitation of the region despite its rich natural resources, such as oil. Why this youth involvement?With their population numbers greater than any other demographic in the country as well as increased access to education and news from across the globe but with no corresponding opportunities to earn a livelihood, many youth are not ready to wait their proverbial turn to lead. They see what life could be, are convinced they have what it takes to take leadership immediately, and are going forward to seek it. This process reverses social order. As Anugwom further shows, this intervention transforms existing social relations of hierarchy and support as "young people transform from those who depend on the guidance and direction of the older generation in the ideal socio-cultural context to those who provide protection and liberation for their communities". The youth see injustice in their communities and are compelled to intervene. Quite often, however, they lack the political or military strength to change the unjust systems oppressing their communities. That does not stop them from mobilizing multiple strategies in the hopes of bringing about positive change to their communities. One of the strategies they employ is drawing power and inspiration from their community's religious repository, specifically the *Egbesu* deity. Considered the source of great traditional strength to protect the Ijaw people against injustice *Egbesu* has been called upon to empower youth to fight the government and multinational oil corporations.Focusing on Egbesu's new fund role as both a protector and energy-giving power for those being attacked and also attacking, Anugwom's project enters into an existing anthropological conversation around the topics of development, modernity, and the occult. These conversations see these topics intersected in complex ways and amplified through intersections of local material realities, spiritual beliefs, and local expectations of progress or "development." Anthropologists working in other African countries have shown the persistence of traditional worldviews in the failure of modernity. Youth in the Niger Delta drawing on *Egbesu* reflect this worldview as an attempt to reverse the state of affairs in their community and also primarily because it is a worldview that considers the spiritual and physical realms to be deeply interconnected. Invoking the occult provides youth in Ijaw and in other locations throughout Africa to redress the inherent inequality in resource distribution. Invoking *Egbesu* as a medium through which to respond to socioeconomic marginalization and exploitation is not a last resort but part of the rhythm of everyday living. If for nothing else youth militants in the Niger Delta can attribute their power and invincibility to *Egbesu*. This book provides a historical account of how and why they accomplish it.

Mwenda Ntarangwi
Vice President,
Theological Books Network,
Grand Rapids, Michigan.

Chapter One

Introduction

Justification and Rationale for the Book

The book argues, on the strength of a thorough-going empirical evidence that in addition to the well-known fact that the oil conflict in the Niger Delta of Nigeria is driven by the youth, these young people have also found it expedient to deploy the powers of the occult i.e. the deity of their society not only in helping them make sense of the perceived marginalization of their society within the political economy of Nigeria but more critically in helping them ameliorate it. In other words, the youth driven conflict over the marginalization of the Niger Delta from the political economy of oil in Nigeria has also privileged the invocation of the *Egbesu* deity of the Ijaw by these young people not only as a symbol of justice but medium through which justice can be attained. Thus, the *Egbesu* beyond claims about its potency re-emerges in the conflict as not only an idiom of justice commonly shared but also as a cultural rallying point and solidarity for the people.

It equally reflects a longing for a return to the pre-colonial norms regarding ownership and access to natural resources and a rejection of the orthodoxy of the right of the state over these resources. Interestingly, despite the background of prevalent Christianity, the deity does not generate tension in beliefs but responds to the critical exigency of the immediate socio-political environment of the people. The invocation of the occult in conflict situations especially by young people in Africa is not really novel as cases in the Congo and Liberia have shown (see, Beneduce, et al; 2006; Ellis, 1999; Jourdan, 2004).

However, while the above instances can be seen as cases of cultural inversion in the heat of conflict, the Niger Delta case examined here approximates the classic case of cultural revision. In this sense, the young people have simply dug into the cultural repertoire of their group in the bid to attain both justice and achieve the support of their wider society whose members can easily comprehend and relate to the perceived powers of the deity which is a commonly held cultural object. Related to the above core arguments is that the role of the occult in the form of the *Egbesu* in the Niger Delta conflict challenges the tendency to hold onto a parochial Euro-American conceptualization of religion in which there is imagined conflict between that which is seen as religion (defined essentially in terms of the world religions) and that seen as belonging to culture (especially the culture of societies outside of the West). Therefore, the occult in this case does not generate conflict in beliefs but rather responds to the socio-economic realities of the people concerned.

In line with the foregoing, the book focuses on the mediating role and impact of occult imagination in the youth's conflict in the oil-rich Niger Delta region of Nigeria. The concept of occult is used in this case in a broad sense to include beliefs and practices associated with the supernatural[1] and as synonymous with sorcery and to some extent witchcraft[2]. Among the Ijaw of the Niger Delta region of Southern Nigeria, the *Egbesu* deity is an embodiment of supernatural beliefs and practices associated with justice and the cause of the oppressed. Therefore, in this frame of reference occult is conceived largely as a neutral religious force that has both the potentials for good

---

[1] The Egbesu deity of the Ijaw ethnic group as a case in point here

[2] Though witchcraft in some groups in contemporary Nigeria – like among Pentecostal churches and other Christian churches in Nigeria – basically invokes evil.

and evil[3]. Within the social environment of this study, the *Egbesu* deity in its unadulterated socio-cultural context is a traditional religious symbol that approximates good and justice and is therefore essentially a manifestation of good for the Ijaw people. It is also seen largely by the people as a potent means of bailing them out of perceived marginalization in the Nigerian state.

However, since 2015 the conflict has resurfaced, anchored now by a new group of young men and women in the same region. The conflict in the region had been anchored by the youth who waged a relentless war against perceived injustice and unfair treatment in the Nigerian polity. The conflict experienced a lull in the period between 2009 and 2015 largely as a result of a partial successful amnesty programme which kicked off in 2009. However, since 2015 the conflict has resurfaced serious anchored now a new group of young men and women in the same region. In spite of this development, the issues in conflict remain the same.

The Niger Delta region in the Southern part of the country is the source of the oil wealth that is the mainstay of the Nigerian economy. In spite of what is acknowledged as the stupendous

---

[3] Without doubt the traditional healer possesses the same supernatural power as the evil witch or those who harness spiritual or supernatural powers to inflict pain or bad outcomes on other members of the society. Interestingly, "traditional healers treat physical and mental ailments by harnessing the same occult forces that witches use, but for good rather than evil - to defend against supernatural harm and sometimes even to retaliate against witches themselves" (Tebbe, 2007: 194). But even more telling and often forgotten is that the word traditional healer which is now popular became so only a couple of decades ago. In other words, traditional healers were originally referred to as witch doctors or white witches. As already mentioned, the change of name or concept as it were derives from both the pejorative nature of the word 'witch' in popular discourse and the advent of new forms of Christianity 'typicalized' by Pentecostalism. The pejorative element in the above derived essentially from the perception that the use of the term 'witch doctor' has a direct connection to the more generalized perception of witch as embodying evil in African societies.

3

oil wealth[4] in that region (see, UNDP, 2006), it is one of the least developed in the country. As a matter of fact, the UNDP (2006) sees the region as representing a development paradox in Nigeria since the level of socio-economic development in the area is grossly inconsistent with the massive oil wealth in it. But even beyond the glaring social, economic and infrastructural impoverishment associated with this region (see, Obi, 2008; Okonta, 2008; Anugwom, 2005; 2007; Okonta and Doughlas, 2001), the citizens of the region perceive a systematic marginalization of the region by the major ethnic groups in control of state power at the centre in Nigeria[5].

A former state governor from that region has alleged that the decline in the derivation principle of revenue allocation was consequent upon the prominence of oil from the region as the main source of foreign exchange earnings for Nigeria and was a conscious effort to undermine the development of the area by the ethnic majority groups (see, Okilo, 1981). This thesis of ethnic majority conspiracy, as one would label it or what is better framed as ethnic majority elites' conspiracy has received endorsement from various key persons and groups in the region

---

[4] According to some sources Nigeria produces an estimated 2.46 million barrels of oil daily and most of these are sold to the United States and other Western Nations (see, Obi, 2008). In fact reports in Dailies in Nigeria indicate that in 2009 the country was exporting average 1.7million barrels of oil to the international market. This means that Nigeria is undoubtedly Africa's largest exporter of oil and massive natural gas production worth about 22 million tons yearly and natural gas exports account for about US$4 billion annually (see, Obi, 2008). In the account of Ude (2000) Nigeria made over US$228 billion from oil exports between 1981 and 1999. This was the era when oil was consistently below US$20 a barrel which would represent a tidy drop now that oil has remained consistently above US$50 a barrel.
[5] Even with the emergence of an Ijaw from Southsouth Nigeria, Goodluck Jonathan as President (2010 – 2015), this frame of reference built over decades of leadership in Nigeria by Northerners is still potent. Also while the Amnesty programme began in 2009 has reduced conflict in the area, the thorny issues raised by the youth especially the derivation contents of revenue allocation; socio-economic impoverishment; shriveled socio-economic space for young people have not been addressed in any systematic or sustainable manner.

(see, Saro-Wiwa, 1995; 1994; Okonta, 2008 etc.). The above scenario has not been helped by the allegation of collusion between the state in Nigeria and Trans-National Oil Corporations (TNOCs) in the country to ensure that the people of the region are deprived the rights to the oil in the region (see, Omeje, 2006) and more worrisome enthrone an environmentally unfriendly oil exploration that now threatens life in the region (see, Anugwom, 2007). As a result of the above and the development disaster which the area resembles, the youth and other members of society in the region see their situation as basically a case of marginalization.

The Niger Delta problem has received a stream of scholarly attention in the last decade. Beside this, a lot of effort has been expended by local and international civil society organizations and multi-lateral development agencies in calling attention to the various dimensions of the Niger Delta situation ranging from human rights abuse, environmental degradation to political de-empowerment and fiscal inequity. However the corpus of literature on the problem or conflict in the region has varied. Thus, the conflict has been attributed to a myriad of causes ranging from revenue allocation or clamour for improved oil revenue (see, Omeje, 2004; Obi, 2001 etc), ecological/environmental devastation arising from oil extraction (see, Naanen, 1995; Okoh, 1996; Anugwom, 2007 etc), to infrastructural decay and neglect, and marginalisation and frustration (see, UNDP, 2006; van Dessel, 1995; Ifeka, 2000; Ukeje, 2001; Ikelegbe, 2005 etc). In spite of the above commendable efforts, not much attention has been paid to what may be called the grey side of the *modus operandi* of the youth militant groups that have waged war in the region.

But more interesting is that whatever has been written in this area has not dealt in depth with the role of the occult or witchcraft in the conflict. In other words, not much attention has been paid to the intricate nexus between oil, occult and youth involvement in the conflict. However, some attempts

5

have been made in this regard (see for instance, Ghazvinian, 2007; Junger, 2007) but these have not offered a detailed and incisive look at the critical role of the occult in what was ordinarily a youth driven conflict over oil resources. Perhaps, partial exceptions in this regard are the articles by Ifeka (2006) and Omeje (2005a). Ifeka (2006) tried to locate the fetish in the violent conduct of youth in Nigeria. However, this account which covered other hotspots of youth violence beside the Niger Delta region presented a very general picture that ends up locating the occult within the tangents of the youth conflict in the Niger Delta since it sees the fetish as basically the outcome of the mystification of political relations. Moreover, the adoption of the concept of fetishization by Ifeka underlines a value-laden approach and a belief that occult practices are in all cases negative. In other words, the analysis suffered from the pangs of Christianity driven morality.

While Omeje's (2005a) work comes closer to the mark, it was largely a statist approach to the occult phenomenon and concentrated more or less on the Egbesu Boys (which he sees as metaphor for a number of Ijaw militant groups engaged in the conflict). Though an impressive array of studies have been carried out on the involvement of youth militias in occult or witchcraft practices during conflict in various parts of Africa (see, Ellis, 1999; Jourdan, 2004; Beneduce et al, 2006) nothing holistic has been attempted in this regard in the youth militants oil-related conflict in the Niger Delta region of Nigeria. This is not to deny the mention of the occult in various other accounts of the conflict (see, for example, Obi, 2008; Eghosa et al, 2007). Thus, the present attempt is a detailed study of the occult phenomenon in the Niger Delta conflict beyond the pioneering deployment of the deity by the Egbesu boys of Africa (EBA). Therefore, the present attempt sees the occult as a generalized and imagined potent influence in the conflict.

Most fundamentally, the study aims at a holistic socio-cultural and neutral examination of the occult represented by the

Egbesu deity in the Conflict. In other words, this study is an in-depth examination of the role of the belief and dependence on the occult in the youth conflict in the Niger Delta region of Nigeria. While the invocation of the occult represented by the *Egbesu* deity may be seen as typical of the normative patterns and religious beliefs of the people, I see its crucial role in emboldening, empowering and engendering the struggle of the youth as mediated by the easily perceivable marginalization of the region within the Nigerian federal system and the critical location of the youth in the border line of the social and demographic composition of the population. The youth in this sense is a transitory, permeable and easily influenced social group in spite of possessing boundless agency in social relations.

The examination of the role of the occult in the Niger Delta violence is equally borne out of my belief that there can never be a holistic narration of the occult or magic which holds true at all times and transcends geographical boundaries in its uniformity. Thus, while increase in cases of revival may be universal or global and result from similar challenges of life, the internal logic (rationale, procedure and justifying beliefs) and ingredients of occult differs from one cultural area to another. Therefore, one shares the assertion that occult phenomena, like all other unique and dynamic human preoccupations need to be studied in their own peculiarities (see, Ranger, 2007).

Social Influences and Agency in the Production and Sustenance of Youth Conflict

In appreciating the role of the occult in the youth conflict in the Niger Delta, it would be wise to understand the nature of the youth as a special demographic and social category in any given society. In this sense, youth is a transitory stage at which so many events and phenomena exert influence and compelling pressure in eliciting or generating some actions and responses from the youth. The lack of experience and the seemingly boundless life often perceived at this stage more often than not dispose the youth to reckless behavior, experimentation and ludicrous orientations including conflict and a belief in the ability to recreate society and attain all possible heights. Some of the influences which act on the youth in contemporary society often predispose them to violence and outward show of bravado which may be considered either foolish or untoward by the older generations. This entails that there is a precariousness and unbridled freedom which in reality bestows on the youth the most possible potentials as agents of change in the society. Apart from the increasing and intimidating influence of the social media, young people are also exposed to the normalcy of violence through the media and in the unfolding realities of their daily social milieu.

In an interesting study of the war situation in the Congo, Beneduce et al (2006) identified exposure to violence through the movies as a critical influence in the creation of both the violent tendency and imitation of violence among young people. Therefore, exposure to violent behavior on the celluloid may be a source of negative behavior in young ones and given the intrusion of this form of media into all nooks and crannies of life, these young people are more often than not captive audiences. The impact of these movies and the countless lurid and indecent exposure and ideas online (the internet) and through social media exert a compelling and instructive influence on youth behavior and attitudinal disposition. This expectation is in line with the classical psychological axiom that behavior is a learnt human response to the environment. Hence, the exposure to violent films and other graphic illustrations of violence do not just create space in the young person's psyche for negative behavior but crucially predisposes a willingness to act out the violence. This natural urge to act out is often simulated in role play of children using guns to imitate the actions captured on films and in the extreme the use of physical violence like karate on other children or peers.

Without doubt these films and their compelling narratives of sheer bravery play on the young people's psychology to assume bravery and mirror the invincibility of the lead actor as attainable in reality. More interesting in understanding the approximation of the deity by the Niger Delta youth as the symbol of invincibility and an avenue through which marginalization or injustice is overcome is that it parallels the dominant narratives in the films where the story line often portrays the lead actor as someone exercising physical prowess and cunning to escape marginalization or attain the goals denied him by others. The above is acutely in tandem with the realities which the young people of the Niger Delta perceive as confronting them. In other words, among the Niger Delta youth the above story is all too familiar and so the urge to expunge the perceived injustice and source of inequity through acts of violence and personal bravado have been developed over the years.

But beyond the lure of associative narratives is the fact that the imitation and urge for recreation of what is seen on the screen reflect strong imageries of admiration for the actors seen on screen by the young people. As a result, "these phenomena do not represent a collective regression, on the contrary the identification with the fanciful 'strongmen' created by the cinema industry, reveals a deep exigency of redefining a new identity and a new social status" (Beneduce, et al, 2006: 37). The position of Beneduce and his colleagues here has been supported by other studies carried out in the U.S, Namibia (The Communications Initiative Network, 2004) and India (Goswami and Kashyap, 2004) which show that negative images in the media predispose youth to negative behavior or a tendency to act out or replicate what is seen.

The peril of the young people in the above regard in Nigeria has ironically not been helped by the impressive growth and success of the Nollywood film industry (reputed to be second now to Hollywood) which has a blinding rate of churning out films. The pervasive effects of piracy which makes these movies cheaply available have invariably meant the exposure of the young people to all sorts of influence peddled in the movies. Ironically, as the market of the Nollywood movies grows, so does its young followers and by implication its deleterious effects on the behavior of these young ones. Therefore, the coincidence between a rising indigenous movies industry and the existing western film market both active in merchandising action movies has meant equally a general youth population exposed to violence and the mental frame which perceives violence as well as the forceful assertion of rights as genuine routes to accessing desirable social outcomes or goals in social relationships.

While the youth as a category face similar problems in all human societies, peculiar social circumstances have the effect of producing specific responses among the youth. In this case, socio-structural limitations or the structure of opportunities and the perceived opportunities for future self-realization impact on how the youth perceive their situation and the action seen as imperative to redefine and restructure the socio-structural realities and the position of the youth. This is much the same in Nigeria as elsewhere where there is limited opportunities and space for realization of opportunities by the youth which are seen as the direct outcome of the prevailing socio-political order.

As Gore and Pratten (2003) argue, the youth in Nigeria due to the severe decline of opportunities for self-development can be seen as having a prolonged period of youth. For them, this reality is captured in the notion of the elongation of youth or 'extended youth' which tries to capture the social dynamics behind youth involvement in conflict in different areas of the nation. They contend that today's youth in Nigeria, as a consequence of the economic reforms of the 1980s and 1990s which had negative impacts on employment and other economic opportunities and squeezed personal networks of patronage created over-stay in this social category which in comparison with other age-set cohorts is supposedly transitory. In other words, the lack of opportunities facilitates a situation where

10

young Nigerians are trapped literally in an endless youth category especially those in this age-bracket since the 1980s which coincided with the period of major economic reforms. The lack of opportunities also creates a critical mass of potential recruits into militant groups. This is especially the case in the Niger Delta of Nigeria where the youth are hard put to reconcile their dire socio-economic situations with the enormous amount of wealth derived from the oil resources in the environment on daily basis. A similar situation incidentally plays out in the Northeast of Nigeria where the Boko Haram insurgence has been related to the prevailing socio-economic privation especially for young people in that zone (see, Comolli, 2015; Loimeier, 2012; Aghedo, 2014).

However, even though dire socio-economic conditions may be generalized for all groups in Nigeria; in the Niger Delta region, it became a most telling and traumatic experience for the younger generation and generated frustration and loathing for the state seen locally as the source of the problem. As already mentioned, the young people in the Niger Delta unlike their peers in the Northeast could not easily reconcile the disconnect between high unemployment and declining economic opportunities and an ever increasing and expanding exploitation of oil resources in their environment especially as they were aware of the high cost of oil in the international market (at least until 2015) and its yield into the national economy. The outcome of the above was the eagerness to be involved in actions deemed necessary for liberation from the stultifying socio-economic situation in the region. In the process of forcefully seeking a resolution of the fundamental irony of their existence, the youth of the region privileged a discourse of marginalization and injustice and saw the *Egbesu* as the mediator of their agency in redressing the situation with the Nigerian government and TNOCs.

Therefore, "youth involvement in the Niger-delta struggle took a decisive turn with the repression suffered in the hands of the Abacha government that turned Niger-delta communities into garrison enclaves patrolled by the Nigerian military" (Osaghae, et al, 2007: 11). Without doubt, government's insensitivity and repressive stance towards the agitation were instrumental in turning its course for the worse. Apart from seeming a realistic alternative, the recourse to violence by the youth may have been motivated by the need to match the arsenal of the military engaged in the region.

Incidentally, youth violence apart from the socio-cultural challenges it generates is usually widespread and endangers generations i.e. it may create a situation whereby successive youth generations perceive violence against the state as the only way to go (incidentally the current upsurge in the conflict after some years of relative peace bears out this fact). This process of portraying violence as a way of life and the inevitable response to social privation engenders the widespread appropriation of violence by other sections of the population. As a result, in the Niger Delta while youth involvement in conflict with government forces and Trans-National Oil Corporations (TNOCs) is well known, the proliferation of violence and youth cults in urban areas of the region have also affected children. As Oruwari and Owei (2006) discovered, though the average age of youth involved in violence and cult activities in Port Harcourt, Rivers state is 24 years, children as young as 8 years of age are often recruited into these cults. Incidentally cradle recruitment by militant groups and urban gangs associated with them implies the contamination of the future of society and complicates the regeneration and recovery of society from such traumatic events as long lasting violent conflict. However, more troubling is that children involved in violence and who have seen it as route for negotiating social and economic resources may resist efforts at weaning them from such ways and more critically portend the likely relapse of the society into disorder in the future.

Another way of understanding the dynamism of youth as a critical category of society is to see this social category as the makers of society. In this sense, the youth contribute to the norms, structural definitions and reshaping of the society through their diverse activities. Therefore, in the process of acting out the above script in the society, the youth also make themselves through inventive forms of self-consciousness, transformation and evolving identities (De Boeck, 1999). The most interesting thing is that the youth while making and transforming themselves also make society. This they do through acting as political force, as sources of resistance and resilience, and as supernatural or ritual agents and generators of morality and healing through masquerade and play (Argenti, 1998). In this sense, the role of the *Egbesu* in the youth conflict in the Niger Delta may be seen as fulfilling the aspirations and desire of the youth to heal, remake and transform their society while embodying the critical age-old agent of justice represented by the deity.

From the foregoing, it is only normal that the youth are most likely than any other demographic group to be in the frontline of agitations for change and new paradigms of social relationship. The youth militants in the Niger Delta largely conform to this expectation and may see their actions as representing and embodying the best intentions of the society. But, while positive youth dynamism may bode well for the growth of society, the involvement of the youth in orgiastic violence and in long lasting conflict may endanger the emergence of the youth as a healthy category of the society especially after conflict. Therefore, the contention that the youth is a tension filled, highly unstable category whose management is of crucial importance for society's stability and development (Osaghae, et al, 2007) is indeed very instructive.

The Permeability of the Youth as a Social Category

It is natural to expect that the decades of conflict and violence in the Niger Delta have eroded the traditional social system; its significance and role in the lives of the youths. In fact, 'with traditional kin-based, ethnic and multigenerational associations that manage the transformations from boyhood to manhood and from girlhood to womanhood having lost their taken-for-granted status and social significance, youths seek new avenues for socialization in form of gangs and their associated multiple subcultures' (Osaghae et al, 2007: 3). Along these lines, the long lasting conflict and struggle in the Niger Delta region have probably confused the imaginations of youth as a social category. Perhaps underlining this belief is the generous application of the notion of youth which often creates a twilight zone that is highly permeable and generates ambiguities that enable opportunistic political elites to change colors at will and in the process pollute the youth space.

The ambiguities implied in the above which is well privileged in the arena of politics portends the diminishing of youth agency and challenges local capacities for positive framing of development in the region. For instance, the shifting conception of the youth was exploited by some state governors of the Niger Delta region during the controversial resource control debates and the legal tussle with the federal government over the interpretation of the operational meaning of the continental shelf of Nigeria in the early 2000s. The desire to appear popular and make political capital out of the then heated tussle led opportunistic politicians into the monkeying of youth (see, Gore and Pratten, 2003).

Conflict influences both the assumption and construction of identity by young people. According to Mbembe (2002), wars can be perceived as a general cultural experience that shapes identity like the family, school and other institutions of society do. What is manifest from the preceding statement is the contradiction between the usual cultural frame of reference before conflict and the violence propelled frame of reference emerging out of conflict. The collision between these two generally present problems of social integration and

14

psychological balance for the youth and even other members of the population. It is a sociological reality that long drawn violent conflicts produce state of normlessness or lack of clear norm reference. Hence, the exposure to militant warfare entails that young people build new bases of identity; cross the line of decorum set by culture; and more critically build new forms of solidarities and engage in new processes of interaction and modalities for accessing valued resources in the society. Part of the process of seeking a niche of alliance with the society in the troubling times of conflict especially with an external enemy is to invoke solidarity with a popular and commonly venerated deity like the *Egbesu*.

Conflict especially when anchored by the young people often catapults them into the position of protectors and defenders of their communities. As a result, young people transform from those who depend on the guidance and direction of the older generation in the ideal socio-cultural context to those who provide protection and liberation for their communities. The feelings of emergency responsibility imbued in this privilege the rationalization of violence and the impunities of violent conflict and often have defining and lasting impact on the social system concerned. This is no less the case in the Niger Delta region of Nigeria where the youth militants assumed responsibilities for protecting and looking after their communities during and even immediately after the conflict. Hence, the youth militants, 'claim to have a liberation agenda and claim to protect the interests of their communities...the interests of the Niger Delta region' (Oruwari and Owei, 2006: 7). The above sentiments often captured even in the narratives of the youth militants themselves generate the imaginations of youth as cultural vanguards. This imagination which seems like cultural inversion may create cognitive confusion that sets in motion ambiguities about the role of youth in peace times and task the rehabilitation of these youth militants after a protracted conflict.

15

Although the use of occult imaginations (represented by the *Egbesu* deity) is quite popular among the youth militants in the Niger Delta and parallel similar deployment of occult imaginations by youth in other conflict zones as evidenced in the Congo and Sudan, the Niger Delta case has some peculiarities that set it aside from the main path of youth in conflict occult narratives in the continent. As Harnischfeger (2006: 57) concluded after a survey of militant groups in different parts of Nigeria, "militias in Nigeria typically make use of magic or spiritual powers". This tendency which is often simply dismissed as a relic of culture or tradition[6] or what Harnischfeger sees as efforts to gain legitimacy has shown in recent times a propensity to embolden militant groups and engender different forms of militant led contestations in various parts of the country. The case of the Niger Delta draws peculiar attention perhaps as a result of the economic importance of the region and the resilience which the conflict led by the youth has exhibited in that region. Also, the above peculiarity can be further captured in the fact that the Niger Delta militants rather than inventing and exploiting new imaginations of the occult have keyed into the prevailing occult imageries within their normative experience. However, they have extended and appropriated this normative experience to suit the exigencies of their marginalization and the oil conflict.

Overview of the Nature of the Occult

Generally the words used in describing occult forces in Africa differ from one language group to another. But in spite of the above, the occult whether seen as *juju; sangoma; djambe; muthi; evu;* or *sem* implies the utilization of supernatural or invisible force for constructive or destructive purposes. For

---

[6] This is often captured in extant literature as a process of retraditionalism

instance, traditional healers, rain makers and traditional leaders are seen as typically deploying occult forces for constructive purposes while other people often invoke such powers for destructive purposes like harming others or for selfish/greedy purposes (like making money or achieving valuable economic or social ends).

Incidentally the typical African cosmology makes a loose distinction between religion (seen loosely here as worship of the supernatural beings in different guises all over Africa) and witchcraft and sorcery (usage of supernatural means or gifts and beliefs in them to achieve control, manipulation of situations and also to achieve selfish and often evil intentions). While witchcraft or sorcery is often invoked for positive ends (healing, prophesying and unraveling mysteries), there is also a widely acknowledged usage of these powers or beliefs in these powers often for negative and even evil purposes. This is one sense in which the idea of the occult becomes pertinent. Related to this is the appropriation of the collectively owned and venerated supernatural force for personal and group ends not subject to collective conscience but rather to the individual's or sub-cultural group's definition and perception of what is wrong and what is right. This process endows a life force, presence and coercive power on the supernatural that can be exploited for individual ends outside the popular notion of religion as a system of beliefs collectively identifiable with diverse social groups. It is in this sense that I adopt the concept of occult in this book to refer to the invocation of supernatural power by the youth militants in the Niger Delta region of Nigeria.

There is no gainsaying the fact that even though we have gone a long way from the Trobriand Islands of Malinowski's time, occult practices or magic still serve to enable men impose control over events or at least achieve the security that comes with some semblance of control and understanding of the external world. In this sense, their allure is found in the control, predictability and understanding they provide as well as fostering man's belief in his ability as a superior being to deal with both problems and the unknown. Little wonder the occult becomes attractive when the individual cannot understand events; when illnesses defy known cures; when events fall outside the realm of known logic; and when life is threatened in one form or another. Therefore, 'magical beliefs and practices, in this view, are to be understood as a set of tools that can be used both to make sense of the mysteries of modern, global life and also to gain some form of control over the external world' (Pile, 2006: 306).

While there is no contesting the fact that the occult as umbrella expression of supernatural and spiritual powers bound within culture may breed analytical ambiguity, the over-emphasis on distinctions can equally breed confusion in the bid to analyze different manifestations of the occult. There is no arguing the fact that even though one may distinguish between the concepts of sorcery, witchcraft and magic at times; at other times such distinctions become very blurred in practical cases. For instance, witchcraft is often seen as purely destructive and secretive utilization of the occult. In the views of Harnischfeger (2006), it typifies the most secret form of occult aggression. But this denotation becomes confusing in some African communities where the emphasis is on black versus white witch. In this case, the white witch is positive and is used in referring to both traditional healers and rain makers (and others who use spiritual or supernatural powers to do good in their communities). In this situation the utility of such distinction becomes more confusing than elucidating. There is also the tendency for witchcraft to be viewed along gender prisms and thus women are depicted as more prone to witchcraft than men. In fact, it is often rationalized that in patriarchal societies where women are denied access to secret institutions and communal bastions of occult, the involvement in witchcraft becomes the option. In spite of the value of the above thinking, it is only tenable where the experience of the occult justifies such distinction in any given situation but not universally the case.

Though the expression 'magic' in modern thought means a number of things ranging from the deceitful guile employed in sponging money off people; the make belief performance of unbelievable feats like cutting a human being into two to the admiration of cash paying viewers of a magic show to the ability to perform extra-ordinary feats like eating fire and chewing bottle in circus shows etc., magic in its original sense still lies within the occult rubric and implies the possession and usage of supernatural powers. Be that as it may, the confusion mentioned with regards to the use of the concept of witchcraft also arises in trying to separate magic from sorcery and vice versa. In fact, in some sweeping sense of usage any expression of supernatural or spiritual powers in modern society which is not traceable to the God of the universal religions is seen simply as witchcraft. It is in view of the above, that I subscribe, in spite of its rudimentary logic only to the basic distinction between positive and negative occult or the use of the occult to the benefits of the larger community as opposed to the utilization of such powers for selfish, destructive and harmful ends by individuals with access to or endowed with such powers.

In spite of the foregoing, the interplay between occult and the actions of the youth militants in the Niger Delta is one that demands careful explanation in order not to arrive at tenuous cause and effect relationship or ascribe consequences to insignificant incidences or display. In other words, the invocation of the occult even when captured as manifestation of religious belief and thus inherently neutral may conjure up imaginations of the irrationality often ascribed to bold actions of the youth population in any society. In this sense, giving too much prominence to occult narratives or ascribing too much powers to them contrary to what can be perceived or established may take away the rational claims of the Niger Delta militants and make bringing back 'civics' (in the views of Okonta, 2008; 2006) a much more difficult exercise.

This does not mean that a people's religion should not be construed as reflecting them or that belief systems are inherently irrational since our very rationality often derives from our beliefs even though we may not be aware of this. But one must refrain from playing into the hands of a few misdirected notions of the conflict in 21st Century Africa as entirely atavistic and senseless. Therefore, it would be interesting to ascertain the extent to which the Niger Delta conflict can be captured in the framework of Donald Snow as 'uncivil war' with no apparent ennobling purpose or outcome (Snow, 1996). This concern should be framed within the context of the role of the occult and how deterministic such role is and its perceived or real effects on the youth as the vanguard of the conflict.

Beyond its immediate examination of the Niger Delta crisis within the occult and youth conflict parameters, the exercise here should be considered as continuation of efforts to understand the oil-conflict nexus in Africa and from this seek explanations why oil cannot foster development in the continent and more critically, how oil (contrary to prevailing experiences in oil dependent economies in the continent) can generate development rather than conflict in Africa. As Afeikhena (2005: 3) makes clear, 'oil has fuelled internecine conflicts. Since year 2000, there has been 29 wars waged in Africa over the control of mineral resources notably oil, many of them in West Africa'. The focus on the occult and how such beliefs and rituals impact on or mediate resource conflict by the youth population may be considered germane to the above broader concern.

Brief on the Method

The book drew its information from the combination of both primary and secondary sources of data. Even though a robust literature exists on the Niger Delta oil conflict I must admit that with regards to the *Egbesu* phenomenon, the literature is almost barren. The use of primary data was beset with the

20

predictable problem of getting respondents to proffer information as well as navigating through the creeks of the two states of Bayelsa and Rivers in the midst of the general insecurity bred by the conflict and the litany of criminal gangs operating under the cover of the insecurity generated by the conflict in these states[7].

The states of Bayelsa and Rivers were chosen simply because of the fact that they boast of a considerable population of the Ijaw which is the ethnic group of the youth militants mainly involved in the conflict as well as the owners of the *Egbesu* deity. In fact, Bayelsa is often seen as an Ijaw state given the overwhelming dominance of the Ijaw ethnic group there. Moreover, the Movement for the Emancipation of the Niger Delta (MEND) which is the main Ijaw dominated militant group and its allies operate more from these two states than any other in the region; so they were locations or theaters of the conflict[8].

Also, the focus on the Ijaw ethnic group is logical in reference to two main facts. In the first place, the Ijaw constitute the largest ethnic group in the Niger Delta region whether one refers to the so-called core Niger Delta states or the nine states that make up the political or constitutional Niger Delta. In the nine states of the Niger Delta, the Ijaw is still the majority since only two Igbo ethnic group states (Imo and Abia) are included in the nine. The Ijaw or *Izon* made up of a loosely affiliated 40 clans have a population of over 10 million and are predominantly located in Bayelsa and Rivers state. But apart from demographic imperatives, the *Egbesu* deity which is my concern here belongs to the Ijaw and it is associated with militant groups from the Ijaw ethnic group.

---

[7] The main bulk of primary data was collected between 2008 and 2009 before the Amnesty programme. The conflict at this period was wide ranging and severe

[8] Interestingly the MEND still disavows the amnesty and rehabilitation programmes of the state

Thus such Ijaw militant groups or groups dominated by the Ijaw like the Egbesu Boys of Africa (EBA); the erstwhile Niger Delta peoples Volunteer Force (NDPVF) led by Asari-Dokubo and the larger than life Movement for the Emancipation of the Niger Delta (MEND) (still active now – 2016- but largely suing for peace and embrace of dialogue by nascent militant groups) can all be associated with the *Egbesu*. In fact, Omeje (2005a: 71) argues, 'the NDVF and a host of other Ijaw – dominated anti-oil militias operating in Nigeria's Niger Delta region are widely believed to be extraordinarily emboldened in their resistance against the state and oil industry because of their collective 'spiritism' and magical paraphernalia of warfare'. In spite of the semantic twist towards the end of the above quotation, Omeje was apparently referring to the belief in the role of the *Egbesu* deity in the conflict.

The study which provided the information for the book all the same benefitted from a strong methodology which I hope facilitated the achievements of the objectives of the book at the end of the day. Be that as it may, the study utilized the triangulation logic in all aspects of its methodology. In this sense, data were collected through four different methods and the analysis was anchored equally on a complementary approach. Data were collected through the following:

a. **Document Review (archival, published, unpublished and grey literature on the Niger Delta crisis):** Quite a lot has been written on the Niger Delta by different authors and from different sources and organizations. In fact, one often gets overwhelmed with the amount of things published in different media about the conflict. Apart from the usual run of the mill sources, there is also the information contained in grey literature accounts. These were often sources of very useful information on some neglected dimensions of the conflict like the occult. There is also quite a good volume of archival materials on the Niger Delta region cataloguing relations among different groups there and the Ijaws and their neighbors in the National Archives in Lagos and Enugu. Equally a lot of things have been written in contemporary times by different media on the Niger Delta conflict; in addition to these are a good number of other materials – press releases, bulletins, reports and flyers from the youth militant organizations, the government, and the oil corporations operating in the Niger Delta. Incidentally, there has been a flourish of literature on occult and witchcraft in modern Africa focusing on diverse aspects of these phenomena. There are also documented accounts of the involvement of youth militias in occult practices in other parts of the African continent. All the above constitute robust documentary materials utilized in various sections of the book.

b. **A combination of the Key Persons Interviews and In-Depth Interviews:** Interviews were conducted with key actors the Niger Delta oil conflict. Basically the researcher utilized the purposive sampling method based on involvement/participation as well as level of participation in the conflict to select respondents for the interviews. In the interviews (which are like the meat of information for the book) I (with my very helpful local research team) focused only on the youth militants identified by our informers as either MEND fighters or members of the other Ijaw groups aligned to the MEND. Apart from the need to have some defined universe of respondents, the choice of MEND fighters is borne out of the recognition that apart from the Egbesu Boys of Africa (EBA) who openly confirmed the role of the *Egbesu* deity in its struggle (see, Omeje, 2005a); the MEND is another group that has openly declared association with and belief in the *Egbesu* deity (see, Ghazivinian 2007; Junger, 2007 for instance).

c. **Focus Group Discussions:** There were six focus group discussions in both states during the months of May and June

2008. The FGDs made up of six members per panel took place in Nembe and Ekeremor in Bayelsa State and Buguma in Rivers State. These were areas where the field workers working with me could establish the atmosphere for FGDs and incidentally are areas with a known prominence of the *Egbesu* deity.

d. Oral tradition survey: This focused on narratives, folklores and popular tales regarding the Ijaw and their *Egbesu* deity from old men and cultural gate-keepers in the areas of study which helped in building some crude ethnography for the study.

While the documentary data from the above sources were subjected to content analysis to derive needed information for the study, descriptive and contextual analysis of the information derived from the interviews and FGDs were carried out. Given the nature of my concern here, the capturing of some critical elements of the past especially the nature and role of the *Egbesu* in traditional Ijaw society entailed that the analysis also employed both diachronic and synchronic approaches in relating and comparing the information collected from the diverse sources utilized.

Structure/Organization of the Book

The book is divided into nine main chapters logically related and flowing from each other. These chapters are built around answering the major research questions which guided the study upon which the book is based. These questions are:

- How has occult imaginations mediated the youth conflict in the oil-rich Niger Delta region of Nigeria?
- To what extent is the occult practice of the youth militants reflective of the Ijaw socio-cultural norms?
- What is the nexus between the occult imagination and the perception of marginalization by the Ijaw people of the Niger Delta region?

- What useful parallels can be drawn between the Niger Delta occult phenomenon and the use of the occult by youth in other conflict areas in Africa?
- To what extent is the peculiar manifestation of the occult in the Niger Delta conflict captured in extant social sciences theories and perspectives?
- What new polemics are thrown up in the larger fields of youth study, religion and occult by the Niger Delta case?

The first chapter of the book is the introduction which is presented in three main sections viz. justification and rationale for the book which details the research problem and observed lacuna in knowledge which makes the work imperative. In fact, the paucity of studies of the occult in contemporary social sciences cannot be easily denied. However, the book is driven by the observation that despite references to the *Egbesu* deity in the analysis of the Niger Delta youth conflict in Nigeria, there has not been a concerted attempt to carry out a holistic study of this phenomenon. Apart from the works of Ifeka (2006) and Omeje (2005a) which were relatively short journal articles and somewhat encumbered by the facts already raised in the first section of this chapter, there is a prevailing air of denial of the occult in the extant literature (see, Obi, 2001 for instance).

Apart from the above, the effort here seems to represent the attempt to join issues with dominant contemporary social science scholarship which often perceives the occult from a value-laden perspective as not religion. Hence, there is need to examine the occult from a neutral perspective and within the context of the lived experience and socio-cultural make-up of a given people in Africa (the Ijaw). The study of the *Egbesu* is also about the spirituality or otherwise of the Ijaw ethnic group in the South south zone or Niger Delta of Nigeria; the *Egbesu* is an Ijaw deity and the discussion of the *Egbesu* is to some undeniable extent a discussion of the Ijaw people. However, while I will not engage in historical narrative of the Ijaw since I'm hardly

25

equipped for such intellectually onerous task; my remit here is to examine the deployment of the *Egbesu* deity by Ijaw youth engaged in conflict over oil resources with the federal government of Nigeria and its agencies.

Undoubtedly the Ijaw commands focus in the discourse of contemporary conflict in the Niger Delta since it is the dominant ethnic group in the region. Apart from this, after the pioneering efforts of the Movement for the Survival of Ogoni People (MOSOP) and Ogoni youth, the conflict in the Niger Delta region has been waged by Ijaw youth and the Ijaw influence in the entire conflict in the region has been massive. The next section gives an overview of the social influences which impact on the youth as agency in the production of conflict; while the last section of this chapter highlights the methodology of the book. In a very short sense, the study adopted methodological triangulation as a guiding principle. This has facilitated the gathering of data from various sources. The only methodological challenge, apart from getting respondents to talk, in view of their concerns for security, arose in the attempt to reconstruct the *Egbesu* deity in its ideal pre-colonial and pre-conflict state. However, this weakness was amply compensated by the massive information gathered in other areas. Finally the last section of this chapter is the one you are reading now which is the description of the structure and nature or contents of the various chapters in the book.

Having established the justification or rationale for book; the next chapter (two) focuses on the context and location of the area of study. In this case an attempt is made in the chapter to achieve a graphic description of the various features and characteristics of the Niger Delta region as well as the dominant political discourse which has contextualized the youth conflict in the region. Thus, apart from giving the geographical location of the region in the larger Nigerian state and the geographical attributes of the Niger Delta; the chapter looks at the Niger Delta as a political discourse in which case in spite of the fact that the delta represents an incontestable geographical fact, the notion of the Niger Delta has been represented especially in formal government spheres beyond the merely geographical. This chapter also looks at the environment and various groups in the Niger Delta i.e. a socio-economic and demographical description of the Niger Delta. The third chapter deals with an interesting focus on the issue of marginalization of the region within the Nigerian nation and how the reality of this marginalization has sponsored imaginations of conspiracy and deliberate subjugation on which the conflict was based. It discusses the narratives of marginalization in the region in three interrelated dimensions and argues that these perceptions of marginalization are critical drivers of the conflict.

The fourth chapter of the book takes an overview of the dominant theories which have been invoked in social sciences scholarship in explaining the really worrisome phenomenon of conflict and conflict over natural resources in different areas of Africa including Nigeria. I also tried here to examine the extant theories of the occult in the African continent as a prelude to locating the Niger Delta phenomenon somewhere within this universe of theories. In order to achieve some form of order, the presentation of the above concerns are organized into three main sections viz. the usual culprits i.e. theories which have employed largely a political economy logic in explaining conflicts in Africa; the economic oriented theories or explanations like the resource curse hypothesis which focus on the economic rationale or motives behind resource conflict in Africa; the social theories or explanations which focus on social relations as explaining conflicts.

There was some careful thinking done before I settled for the title of this work. This thinking resulted from acknowledgement of the ambivalent conceptualizations of such concepts like witchcraft, occult, sorcery and religion in the extant literature. A very good representation of this type of discourse in the literature is the rebuttal of the notion of occult that ter

Haar and Ellis (2009) saw in an article by Terence Ranger (Ranger, 2007). While these sentiments are later taken up in this volume, the fact is that there is more or less a division among scholars on whether the notion of occult is inherently negative or neutral and more crucially whether categories like occult, witchcraft and sorcery can be labeled religion or not. The above issues form the basis of the chapter five of the book which is titled, 'Debate with Religion'. The chapter looks at what is religion, the nature of religion and the place of the occult in the foregoing. Part of the controversy in regarding the occult or witchcraft as religion is that as Geschiere (1997), points out people usually associate those things with the historical past of Africa. In other words, they are anachronistic to modernity or contemporary realities as we know them.

While the above thinking has its allure without doubt, it has not eradicated these beliefs or practices in today's Africa. In other words, instead of being relics of the past these phenomena are often maneuvered in subtle and often intrusive manners into our consciousness in the so called modern age. Thus, in Africa an individual in spite of his education, western paraphernalia and social distance from tradition has often had to negotiate the occult whether defined in terms of the animosity one encounters in the office; the fear of spending time in the village; drinking in pubs; not leaving your drink to ease yourself in a public gathering or in the more raucous invocation of the power over such phenomena by the new Pentecostal churches springing up alarmingly all over Africa. However, while the treatment of the occult as negative and outside the realm of religion may find support in contemporary Christian and popular discourses, I find this really unhistorical and akin to the separation of such phenomenon from the socio-cultural domain where it rightly belongs. Therefore, I treat the occult here neutrally as a manifestation of the religion of the people and which may portend both negative and positive dimensions depending on usage and the perspective of the person doing the interpretation.

The next chapter (six) is built essentially on the information gathered from the field (mainly the interviews and ethnographic data) and focuses on the different forms and nature of the manifestation and usage of the *Egbesu* by the youth militants in the Niger Delta. This chapter aims to achieve two main tasks in addition to the description of the *Egbesu* viz. the extent to which the use of the *Egbesu* in the conflict by the youth resembles the ideal roles prescribed or imagined by the tradition for the deity among the Ijaw people; following this is to ascertain if the deployment of the deity by the youth in the conflict resembles a case of the inversion of culture or the revision of culture. Related to the above concern is to see if the imagination of deprivation or marginalization has impacted on the apparent re-invention of the deity by the youth and in that case how has the imaginary of the deity become privileged by or through the socio-economic marginalization of the region in Nigeria. These form the focus of the chapter seven of the book.

The penultimate chapter (eight) of the book is an attempt to relate the deployment of the deity by the youth militants in the Niger Delta to similar or parallel cases in other conflict areas in Africa. Incidentally quite an appreciable volume of literature exists on such conflicts in the Congo, Liberia, Sierra Leone and even Sudan. The chapter also looks at the impact of the involvement in the conflict and use of the occult on the youth and the socio-economic implosion which predisposed the youth in the Niger Delta to conflict. But more critically from a sociological point of view, is how the conflict and the active engagement of the younger generation invoke both role reversal and portends socio-cultural fluidity that goes beyond the conflict period. In other words, how do conflict and the deployment of the occult implicate a socio-cultural reconstruction of the youth as a category in the society?

Finally, in the last chapter of the book, I attempt some conclusion especially on the reality or otherwise of the vitality of the deity in the Niger conflict in Nigeria as well as the implication of the evidence from the study on the studies of youth agency, involvement of the youth in violence and critically whether the occult category in this case is analytically valuable. In a postmodern speak; this chapter also tries a deconstruction of the occult in the conflict. In addition to this, the chapter equally recaps the major issues addressed in the book; make conclusive statements on the major concerns (as encapsulated in the objectives) of the book; addresses the theoretical question again in view of the findings from the field and venture some recommendations for further studies in the area of youth studies and religion.

Chapter Two

The Niger Delta of Nigeria: Context and Location

The Geographical Niger Delta

The Niger Delta of Nigeria is regarded as one of the world's largest wetlands and invariably the largest in Africa. In this sense, it constitutes 20,000 square kilometers and is a flood plain resulting from the accumulation of centuries of silt washed down the Niger and Benue Rivers in Nigeria (see, HRW, 1999). The Niger Delta region is made up of four main ecological zones – coastal barrier islands, mangroves, fresh water swamp forests, and lowland forests. According to Phil-Eze and Okoro (2007), the Niger Delta has the largest and most important mangrove forest in Africa as well as the third largest in the world and harbours a high diversity of flora and fauna – including endemic, endangered and threatened species.

Also the fresh water swamp forests of the Niger Delta reach over 11,700 km^2 and has a high and rich biodiversity made up of extensive swamps and forests as already indicated (see, World Bank, 1995; Jones, 1998; Omeje, 2006; Phil-Eze, 2001; NDDC, 2004 etc.). However, the above rich biodiversity is under severe threat from diverse sources such as deforestation, oil and gas exploitation, urban growth and environmentally unsound farming methods resulting from encroaching land degradation from oil activities that continuously limit the land space available for any other purpose.

But equally important is that the Niger Delta with an estimated 400km^2 coastline accounts for over half of Nigeria's coastline. It is an area also inundated by various creeks, small rivers, inland waterways and dense forests and under-growths which makes local knowledge very important for activities in the area. The Niger Delta region has a population of over 36 million (using recent projections) people in the nine constituent states of Abia, Akwa Ibom, Bayelsa, Cross River, Delta, Edo, Imo, Ondo and Rivers (see map). However, due to the contested and highly politicised nature of the Niger Delta both as a concept and social reality, there is often a distinction between the so-called *core Niger Delta* and other areas of the region. In this case, the core Niger Delta would imply the states of Akwa Ibom, Bayelsa, Delta, and Rivers which incidentally are the areas with high off-shore oil activities. Also quite recently, the concept of *'coastal states*[9]' has been invented by the government in a half-smart and what may be seen as ethnic moves to appease the South-south minorities in the Region. In spite of the above political modifications, I use it in this study in its geo-political sense to refer to the nine states above which is also in tune with the spirit of the law in Nigeria.

There are a total of 185 local government areas, 40 ethnic groups[10] speaking over 250 indigenous dialects and over 5,000 identifiable communities out of which an estimated 1,500 play host to oil operations or activities of one kind or another. As a result, thousands of miles of oil pipelines crisscross the mangrove creeks of the area interspersed with gas flaring points adding its deadly fumes to an already polluted environment. Perhaps, the only other addition to the above background is the fact that the region is characterized by a massive and pervasive poverty, dearth of social amenities and physical infrastructure. Therefore, despite their location in the petro-lands, oil producing delta states fall below the national average in almost

---

[9] The idea of coastal states would mean the removal of the two South-east oil bearing states (Abia and Imo) and Edo in the South-south from the oil states in Nigeria in spite of the fact that there are large oil deposits in these states

[10] Prominent ethnic groups in this region include the Ijaw, Itsekiri, Igbo, Ibibio, Efik, Ogoni, Urhobo etc.

every measure of social and economic development (Lubeck, et al, 2007; CDD, 2007). But the Niger Delta (as at the time of the original field work for the book in 2008 and now) at night conveys a good impression of the desolation and ruin that the area has become. Thus, most times in the night, the only sign of light comes from flares burning out unwanted gas and causing massive pollution in the environment.

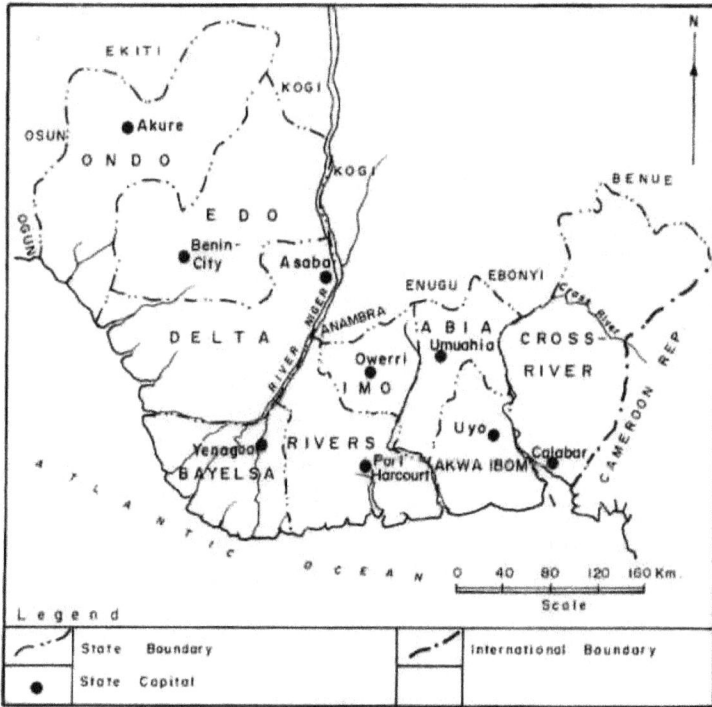

Fig 2 :   Map   of   the   Niger   Delta   States.

Pattern of Environmental Degradation from Oil Activities in the Niger Delta

Incidentally quite a lot has been written on the environmental implications of oil exploitation, which began in the region in 1958 with the sinking of the first oil well at Oloibiri

33

by Shell, ranging from the nature of environmental problems, culpability for environmental damages to consequences that it would not delay us here unnecessarily beyond a brief overview. The environmental problems in the Niger Delta region result mainly from oil spillage, gas flaring, chemical discharge from oil and related activities, and deforestation. Hence, since the discovery of oil in commercial quantity in the 1950s the communities with oil deposits have been suffering various manners of environmental degradation resulting from oil activities. The environmental degradation and the implications for the rights of the people both to a safe environment and meaningful livelihood within their environment have been the cause of recurrent conflict and tension between the people and the government/trans-national oil corporations (TNOCs) (Anugwom, 2014).

For instance, it is estimated that there has been over 4,000 oil spills in the region between 1960 and 2003 while gas flaring from oil extraction has created serious air pollution in the area (EIA, 2003). In 2010, it was reported that between 9 and 13 million barrels of oil has been spilled into the Niger Delta ecosystem due to oil activities (Baird, 2010). Giving a more definite measure to the year spill incidences in the Niger Delta, is the contention of Ordinioha and Brisibe (2013) that on the average about 240,000 barrels of crude oil are spilled in the Niger Delta every year as a result of multiple causes ranging from third-party activities to mechanical failures.

But more insightful is that a study by the Institute for Pollution Studies in Port Harcourt gives a figure of more than 6,000 oil spills totaling more than 4 million barrels between 1976 and 1999 (IRIN, 2002). But equally important in assessing the above figure is that the heightening of oil exploitation since the mid-1980s has invariably meant more spills and gas flaring, where Nigeria is without any doubt the world champion.

Typical Gas Flaring in the Niger Delta

Source: BBC News, Monday 20 February 2006

Oil spills, as any accurate assessment would show result more from the fault of the TNOCs than otherwise. While the cases of sabotage either as protest especially when seeking compensation or as a result of bunkering occur regularly, massive spills and large scale environmental hazards are mainly attributable to the activities of the oil firms. Basically, the oil pipes are more often than not in poor condition and are not replaced as frequently as should be the case. A leader of thought in Nembe is of the view that the oil firms "are mostly using the original pipes they laid over three decades ago and as such corrosion is a major problem. The oil firms because of the corruption in Nigeria are often not in a hurry to abide by international standards of safety in their operations. In fact, it was only recently that they began to show a little concern for what the scramble for oil has done in our communities"[11]. The above is largely corroborated by the report that Shell for instance, continues to use obsolete facilities, corrupting community engagement tactics, the outcome of which has been

---

[11] (Personal Interview, 8 March 2007)

that oil spills and blow-out have become routine (see, ERA/FoEN, 2005).

It is important to understand that though direct environmental problems from oil activities are seen as having moderate priority; the other problems with high priority like bio-diversity decline, fisheries decline, conflict, forest loss, crime and inadequate compensation are either direct outcomes of the oil activities or responses fostered by the oil activities (see, Azaiki, 2003). But more critical is the observation that, 'in spite of the history of oil spills in Nigeria and the provisions of the relevant laws, no oil company has ever been seriously sanctioned or prosecuted for negligence by any environment regulatory agency' (Obi, 1999: 5). A notable exception so far to this was the case in March, 2003 when Shell was ordered by a government committee to pay over $1.5billion to the Ijaw ethnic group for the company's actions in Bayelsa state for over 50 years (see, EIA, 2003)[12]. The same oil company has been indicted by the United Nations Environment Programme (UNEP) Report (2011) much recently for the excess damage of the Ogoni environment by oil exploration. There are currently (2016) serious efforts at the remediation of the Ogoni environment championed by the Federal Government, Shell and the UNEP. In spite of the official launch of this oil spill remediation exercise in Ogoniland, it is expected that this operation would take up to thirty years to be concluded (see, Lazzeri, 2016).

The overall physical environment portrayed above has influenced the social environment in terms of the agitation of the people of the region against perceived environmental abuse resulting from oil exploitation. While the people of the region are itinerant on a local level or within their immediate milieu, the negative response of the state to their agitation has ironically exposed them to wide travels that has invariably influenced both

---

[12] The clean-up of the Ogoni environment was recently launched by the Federal Government of Nigeria (2016)

their perception and response to the environment. Travel generally aids development of new vistas on existing conditions and produced the elites who radically transformed the issues in contention[13] in the region. Therefore, travel offered the elites the opportunity to engage and equally detach from their physical environment which offered them new perspectives. It is in this light that travel occupies a historical watershed in the Niger Delta crisis. Two historical milestones in this regard are worth mentioning.

The first as already hinted is that the punitive response of the state in Nigeria to the agitation of the Ogoni in the 1990s led to the massive exodus of the Ogoni to various parts of the world where they were often easily accepted as political refugees. Second was the historic two million people march in Abuja in 1998 organised by the amorphous organization - Youths Earnestly Ask for Abuja (YEAA). The march which ostensibly was organised to show the support of Nigerian youth for the transformation of the late Sani Abacha the military Head of State then to a civilian Head of State enabled the storming into Abuja of young people from various parts of the country including the Niger Delta. Some of these people were coming to the pristine capital of Nigeria for the first time. For those of them from the Niger Delta, it was a development shock as the splendour of Abuja contradicted sharply with the blight of the Niger Delta region. After this particular travel experience, it became common in popular discourse in the Niger Delta that the wealth from the region has been taken to transform an almost arid land space in Northern Nigeria into a paradise while the region from which the wealth is gotten has been left desolate. The above strengthened the solidarity of the Niger Delta youth and opened their eyes to the degree of deprivation suffered by their people. In summary, these travels provided opportunities for the youth

---

13 Ken Saro-Wiwa as symbolic of this process of building new political consciousness (see his own transformation from the political right to left in Nigeria).

of the Niger Delta to redefine their imagery as well as forge alliances and solidarities.

The People of the Niger Delta

A familiarity with the various creeks, villages and settlements in the Niger Delta region would produce feelings of empathy even from the most ardent supporter of government policies in the region. Such feelings are products of the unimaginable level of poverty, destitution and hopelessness in most of the region' which occasionally may drive the citizens especially the youth to the brink. In fact, the UNDP (2006: 14) succinctly captures this picture of desolation, 'for most people, progress and hope, much less prosperity remain out of reach. Instead, misdirected resources, inappropriate policy frameworks and a poor "visioning" of what development should look like have destabilized their societies and stoked deep and proliferating concerns'. It is likely that the above scenario stokes the embers of discord and aggression from the general populace of the area especially the youth who can hardly envisage any meaningful escape from what appears a doomed existence.

In fact, an observer who visited Yenegoa the capital of Bayelsa state in the region could not understand why a 'community blessed with oil riches under its soil could look as impoverished as Yenegoa in the Nigerian state of Bayelsa' (Woods, 2006: 1). Incidentally, the state has not changed much from the above picture in the ten years period since this visit. Thus, it is this picture of neglect that may give credence to thinking of a systematic project of neglect by the Nigerian state. It might be the perception of this that has bred an enduring discord between civil society in the region and the Nigerian state.

A very important issue in discussing the nature of environmental degradation from oil activities is the nature of legislations or laws guiding the operations of the TNOCs in the area. As obvious in the extant literature, there has been quite a good number of regulations and regulating agencies regarding oil exploitation in the Niger Delta (see, HRW, 1999; Omeje, 2006; FEPA, 1991, etc and Azaiki, 2003 for a full discussion). The plethora of rules in this regard include the Oil in Navigable Waters Act of 1968 which core provision is that it permitted the discharge of hazardous substances or petroleum under certain circumstances, 'such as if the escape of oil from a vessel was due to leakage and the leakage was not due to any want of reasonable care and all reasonable steps have been taken to stop or reduce the discharge' (Omeje, 2006: 44). As is the characteristic of most subsequent laws in the sector, this law is as general as it is ambiguous and largely unenforceable. Little wonder the discharge of what is called un-harmful quantity of effluents in the environment is still practiced in the Niger Delta region today. Currently, there is still talk in the national assembly in Nigeria about the passage into law of the Petroleum Industry Bill (PIB) which would respond in some measures to the needs of the communities in the Niger Delta region to be involved in the oil exploration processes and for more friendly, enforced and strictly regulated exploitation regime that would take cognizance of both the environment and the needs of the people. The Bill when passed into law (a process that is going towards a decade now) would (expectedly) seriously improve the local content or local (Nigerians) participation in the oil sector.

Interestingly, the environmental issue also affects the travel patterns of the people from the core Niger Delta region. In this sense, in spite of the noted commensality and nexus between the rural and urban dwellers in the Southern part of Nigeria, indigenes of the area that are urban dwellers generally make what may be called a flag stop in their villages. The most common practice is that they nestle in a nearby urban area, like Port Harcourt for instance and only rush to spend a few hours in their villages especially during festive periods like Christmas or Easter. The point is that the dearth of basic amenities in the rural areas and the general insecurity prevailing in these areas make the rural areas or villages unfavorable stops for indigenes that live in such urban areas as Port Harcourt, Lagos, Abuja and elsewhere in the world. In fact, this practice was mentioned by one of our respondents, who works in an oil services firm in Port Harcourt. According to him, "I cannot remember the last time I slept in the village willingly with my family. May be I could manage it but my children cannot and I cannot just punish them for no just cause. The whole area is barren with no basic amenities like water, light, good road, you know. What will the children be doing in such a place all day long"[14].

Brief Ethnography of the Ijaw

It would amount to gross naivety or crass arrogance on my part to presuppose I could study a cultural element of the Ijaw people represented in the *Egbesu* deity without an overview of the ethnography of the people concerned. Incidentally quite a lot of the history and cultural narratives of this group in the Niger Delta of Nigeria is best left for professional historians and anthropologists who have worked assiduously in this area of Nigeria. Perhaps, most prominent of these people in contemporary Nigeria are scholars like Obaro Ikime and E.J Alagoa. Therefore, my effort here is not to achieve the level of insightful and detailed description associated with these scholars but to outline the ethnography of the Ijaw ethnic group in the Niger Delta region of Nigeria that would help the reader properly situate the *Egbesu* deity within the socio-cultural heritage and world view of this social group in Nigeria.

The Ijaw (also *Ijo*; *Iẓon*) is a collection of people found mostly in the forest regions of today's Bayelsa (with the largest population and highest number of Ijaw groups or clans); Delta and Rivers States and to a lesser extent in Edo; Ondo; Akwa

---

[14] Personal Interview, 8 March 2007, Port Harcourt Rivers State (extracted from fieldwork notes for an earlier project).

Ibom States all in the Niger Delta of Nigeria. The Ijaw are by nature itinerant fishermen and merchants and thus migrant Ijaw fishermen camps are sited in as far West as Sierra Leone and as far East as Gabon along the West Africa coastlines. However these camps are not permanent settlements though this may change with time. The Ijaw speak about nine closely related languages and a couple of dialects within the *Ijoid* branch of the Niger-Congo language group. The main noticeable language division within the Ijaw is between what is called the Eastern Ijaw (mainly Izon) and the Western Ijaw (mainly Kalabari). These terms are applied mainly to differentiate between geographical locations: the West are located in the western axis of the Niger Delta while the East are located in the Eastern axis of the Niger Delta. So Kalabari is the name of one of the major clans of the Ijaw which inhabit the Eastern axis of the Niger Delta. This group also includes Abonnema, Buguma, Bakana, Degema; and of course the other major groups: Okrika and the Ibani (Bonny, Finima and Opobo).

As obvious from the above, the general language of the Ijaw ethnic group is *Ijo* (often synonymous in pronunciation and spelling with Ijaw which is more of an Anglicized version of the name). While the *Ijo* language is not as big as those of its neighbors like the Igbo and Yoruba and has not really been definitely classified by linguists, it appears to have existed as a separate language from these other neighboring languages for at least five thousand years (see Alagoa, 1999). However, the above fact seems interesting in the sense that:

> This linguistic evidence suggests that theories deriving the Ijo from any of these major ethnic groups as a result of migrations into the delta in comparatively recent times cannot be accepted. It is clear that the Ijo have existed as a separate group, and in the Niger Delta, for a very long time indeed. Their complete assimilation to the peculiar delta

environment is additional support to this view (Alagoa, 1999:
68).

The 40 Clans of the Ijaw* and their Present States in Nigeria

State	Clans
Akwa Ibom	Andoni (obolo),
Bayelsa	Akassa, Apoi Eastern, Bassan, Boma (Bumo, Bomo), Buseni (Biseni), Ekeremor (Operemor), Ekpetiama, Epie-Atissa, Gbaran, Kolokuma, Nembe, Ogbia, Okordia (Akita), Ogboin, Olodiama East, Opokuma, Oporoma, Oruma (Tugbene), Oyakiri (Beni), Tarakiri East, Tungbo, Zarama
Delta	Tarakiri West, Egbema, Gbaranmatu, Iduwini, Isaba, Kabo (Kabowei), Kumbo (Kumbowei), Mein, Obotebe, Ogbe (Ogbe-Ijoh), Ogulagha, Seimbiri, Tuomo
Edo	Egbema, Furupagha, Olodiama West, Ukomu
Ondo	Apoi Western, Arogbo
Rivers	Andoni, Bille (Bili), Bonny (Ibani, Ubani), Engenni (Ngeni), Kalabari, Kula, Nkoro, Okrika (Wakirike), Opobo,

*These are the 40 clans that feature regularly both in grey and published literature and in official government publications. Given the great extensiveness of the group and its highly mobile nature, one would not be totally surprised to see a few more clans apart from those above.

Incidentally there is undoubtedly a variation in socio-cultural patterns and practices between the Ijo and their big neighbours

– the Igbo, Yoruba, Edo. Moreover, as anyone familiar with the Ijaw would readily agree, the group reflects peculiar oral traditions that cannot be realistically related to these other groups especially the Yoruba and Igbo. Perhaps a critical aspect of this reality is the dexterity and deftness which have characterized the Ijaw adaptation to the treacherous littoral portions of the Niger Delta region. Alagoa (1999) equally asserts that the Ijo oral traditions indicate no plausible place of origin outside the delta, but rather capture extensive migrations over the length and breadth of the Niger Delta region by the Ijo. The ease of habitation exhibited by the Ijaw and the dispersal of the group all through the delta amply support the above view.

One thing historians are agreed on is that the Ijaw have various histories of origin. However, while there is no consensus on exactly where the first Ijo took off from, there is no contention that the central ijo area was the point from which further Ijo migrations originated. As Ikime (1999) makes clear though Beni (Benin in present Edo) is mentioned in traditions of origin of the Ijo, though it is not seen as a place of primary or immediate origin. Interestingly, as Ikime equally records, the name Ijo as associated with an eponymous ancestor who migrated from Beni is mentioned only in Beni oral tradition. Therefore, the survey of the oral traditions of the Ijaw would indicate that the central area of the delta was the heartland from which various Ijo groups migrated to outlying regions of the delta (see, Alagoa, 1972).

These central areas from which migrations proceeded, according to Alagoa include Ogobiri, Ikibiri, Oporoma, the Apo Creek and Obiama and other places like Ke, Oboloma (Nembe) in the eastern delta and Oproza in the west of the delta which were centres of secondary migration of Ijo groups (see, Alagoa, 1999). Without over-stressing the point, the Ijo groups' settlement patterns were affected by both their nature as very mobile and transient water dependent groups who were also often constrained by the inability to survive on the mainland and

43

the hostility of hinterland neighbours. While the various Ijo groups migrated from a central heartland and other areas of further secondary migration, the migratory trends differed between the eastern and western delta groups. For instance, there were migrations from Obiama and Itsekiri kingdom of Warri in the west of the delta; the founders of the states of Elem Kalabari and Bonny are probably located in the area between Ogobiri and Kolokuma territory; and the migrations from the centre to the eastern delta is estimated to have happened over a thousand years ago (see, Alagoa, 1999; 1972; 1970)[15].

Alagoa (1999) makes clear that the vast migration of Ijo groups out of the central heartland to other areas also entailed an economic change which incidentally makes the present pollution of the Niger Delta environment (especially severe threats to water resources) through oil exploitation life threatening. As familiarity with the Niger Delta topography would establish, the migration from the central delta to other areas meant equally a movement from a fresh water delta environment to a salt water swamp environment and this entailed a necessary change from a farming economy with supplementary fishing to an economy solely dependent on fishing and salt from the water. But as Alagoa (1999: 70) narrated, 'this change was determined by the fact that the area of the eastern delta was largely under water, and there was little settlement land, and even less for farming. Settlers in this region had by necessity to depend on fishing and the manufacture of salt'.

The Ijo then exchanged these articles with products coming from surrounding hinterland groups. In other words, a large portion of the Ijo land was dependent on the abundant waters there for survival and livelihood. The intense exploitation of oil in these areas since the late 1950s has meant invariably a threat

---

[15] Anyone interested in the detailed history and ethnography of the Ijaw can look up these works of Alagoa who is undoubtedly a leading authority on Ijo history.

to the ability of the group to survive in its environment. In fact, as Azaiki (2003) has argued, the outcome of pollution emanating from oil exploitation has been the severe degradation of both flora and fauna in the entire Niger Delta. The reality and ominous nature of the threat to survival have served as anchors of the exceptional determination of the Niger Delta people to change their situation by any means possible including the use of violence as typified by the waging of wars by youth militants on oil facilities and personnel in the region.

Perhaps, the four most popular delta states going by historical pedigree are Nembe (Brass); Elem Kalabari; Bonny; and Okrika. These states were very active in the pre-colonial contact trade in slaves. These four towns had been referred to as city-states and trading states (Alagoa, 1999). The deep involvement of these states in various trades with Europeans in the pre-colonial era affected the evolvement of social institutions in them. In effect, a majority of social institutions in these areas were developed as a result of the influence of the external trade or commercial links with Europeans. However, overwhelming in the course of development of these institutions were the Ijo culture and the riverine topography of the delta. A remarkable development in the history of traditional authority and governance in the delta states is the transformation of the original house system of authority which favours the oldest male member as leader to the extensive kingship institutions which drew impetus for growth from the massive spread of external trade; the necessity of conflict with neighbours often engendered by disagreement over trading rights; border disputes and rights over fishing water.

The above changes are perhaps more obvious in the eastern and western delta areas which faced different environmental realities from the central delta. In these areas, the *Amanyanabo* who is the head of the lineage which first discovered the scarce piece of settlement land (see, Alagoa, 1999) implies proprietorship and assumes an office endowed with greater

45

political and social authority than the *Amaokosowei* of the village elders of the central delta. At first, the *Amanyanabo* was more or less like informal presidency of the village assembly but the prominence of the towns related to growing trade as well as issues arising from this catapulted the *Amanyanabo* into kingship with power to exercise authority as the prime representative of the community.

Like most other riverine areas in Nigeria, the first European traders in the delta were the Portuguese who used the area as both landing areas and passage way for carrying slaves across the Atlantic into Europe. The Portuguese bought slaves and local food and equally introduced food crops like maize and cassava from South America into the delta. Later European traders include the Dutch, French and the British who eventually developed the colonial system. It is important to point out that apart from the trade related conflicts between the delta and their hinterland neighbors, there was also rivalry and conflict amongst the various delta states over trading rights and privileges. In fact, the emergence of rich trading houses and the city-states like Bonny, Opobo, Brass etc. built around them may be seen as the onset of the conflict over resources in the region. Thus, as aptly captured by Obi (2006: 14):

> There was also the rivalry between city-states, often rooted in the struggle over lucrative trade routes, or for the control of such routes. The control of such routes was a veritable source of revenue or immense wealth either through the collection of tolls or *comey* on the goods that passed through their territory, or by direct participation as middlemen or traders in the trans-Atlantic trade.

In this sense, the growth of effective and powerful kingships was buoyed up by increasing external trade which privileged the emergence of dynasties (ruling houses) in these states and contestations over succession and political power. Predictably, families or individuals in the royal lineages that had accumulated resources from the trade often became rallying influences in leadership especially when there are severe threats from outside. As Alagoa and Fombo (1972), showed the case of the Bonny kingdom is emblematic of the above tendency. As a result of a protracted war with the Andoni (a neighboring kingdom) King Awusa had to hand over the reins of power in the Bonny kingdom to Perekule (Pepple) who having made money in the trade was seen as having the wealth and capacity to stem the Andoni challenge successfully. The above scenario or similar scenarios occurred in some other places in the delta and in some cases like the Bonny example above where the direct descendants of Pepple still hold the reins of power effectively created new and enduring dynasties.

As already stated, the Ijaw are seen as traditionally fishermen and farmers[16]. However, the Ijaw as the foregoing narration suggests were one of the first groups in pre-colonial Nigeria to have contact with the white men and thus were heavily involved in trade with the early Europeans and acted as go-between in the trade between these Europeans and the peoples of the interior or hinterlands. In fact, the emergence of the kin-based trading lineages known as "Houses" (later ruling houses and dynasties) among the Ijaw owes its origin to the flourishing trade with early Europeans. These trading houses functioned more or less as crude business corporations and each had a designated leader and a fleet of war canoes for protecting its trade routes and rights and of course for fighting off encroachment from other groups or houses.

However, the occupational profile of the Ijaw has changed considerably over time. Such change can be attributed to a number of factors ranging from general development, education, migration to the maritime nature of the area, and the

---

[16] Farming paddy rice; cultivating plantains, yams, bananas and cocoyam as well as vegetables and tropical fruits like guava, mango, paw-paw, pineapple, oranges etc.

negative impact of oil exploration on the environment which has limited dependence on the eco-system for livelihood[17]. Given the location of the group in the riverine areas, the people are natural maritime professionals; so quite a good number of the Ijaw people became employed in the merchant shipping sector right from the pre-independence days. Today, the Ijaw are still found in maritime occupations; in the civil service especially in the two states of Bayelsa and Rivers and also in the federal civil service and parastatals. The embrace of education by the people helped by extensive government sponsored scholarships especially in the 1970s to early 1990s has created a large number of Ijaw professionals both at home and in the Diaspora. In spite of the above modern occupations, the Ijaw are still people to who fishing and farming are important vocations especially for those in the rural enclaves and those who are marginal to the socio-economic spheres of life in general. The area still produces a significant portion of the seafood consumed in Nigeria. For the people therefore, the destruction of the environment occasioned by extensive and largely environment unfriendly oil explorations have meant the denial of sustainable means of livelihood.

The history and social development of the Ijaw of the Niger Delta shows the people as dynamic and ever responsive to external influences. Such responses have meant often finding new uses for old practices and institutions as well as the evolvement of new social patterns for dealing with exigencies of the time. Even in the colonial and subsequent independence eras, the delta has remained a highly dynamic society characterized by a high level of political consciousness. In spite of the above, changes and responses of the Ijaw group to external influences have been anchored squarely on the ideal Ijo

---

[17] In other words, fishing and farming activities have been grossly undermined by years of pollution which has adversely affected both flora and fauna in the Ijaw enclaves).

48

culture and the demands of the precarious physical environment inhabited by the people.

Be that as it may, my focus in this book on the influence of the *Egbesu* does not mean that the Ijaw are not modern day Christians. Actually as at now over 90 per cent of the Ijaw profess Christianity though the widespread invocation and belief in the *Egbesu* deity among the youth militants portray the axiom that there is a wide difference between confessing Christianity and actually 'living Christianity'. Moreover, as our investigations revealed there is the tendency of compartmentalization of beliefs which is not a peculiar Ijaw thing but quite common among other groups. In this situation, the *Egbesu* exists in its own compartment as the deity of justice and war while God remains unchallenged as the overall Supreme Being. Also, even till now the traditional religious practices of the Ijaw centre around "water spirits" in the River Niger and its tributaries. In addition to the water spirits is a remarkable ancestor veneration that crosses even the boundaries of Christianity among the people. The above religious inclinations are often mirrored in social ceremonies and even funeral ceremonies that are sometimes elaborate, colourful and quite enthralling.

The point is that in spite of the growing number of Christians in the area the Ijaw have elaborate traditional religious practices and observances which often obliterate the lines supposedly set by modern religious beliefs. Generally, water spirits and ancestors are highly regarded and venerated in this traditional religion. The water spirit known as "Owuamapu" occupy a critical and extremely important position in the Ijaw religious pantheon. Associated with the above is the veneration of ancestors and the practice of divination which is widespread. A common form of divination is the practice of "Igbadai" which essentially entails the invocation of the spirits of the recently deceased for interrogations over cause of their deaths or who caused their deaths. This divination is especially used where the nature of death is perceived as either strange or unnatural.

A good insight into the Egbesu deity and its significance can probably be provided by the understanding that in the Ijaw traditional religious beliefs, water spirits are like humans in the sense that they are assumed to have both strengths and weaknesses; and that human beings usually dwelt among the water spirits world before being born into the world. In other words, the water spirits represent both the unborn humans and the distinguished dead. Another critical aspect of the Ijaw traditional religious belief system which may have also informed the popularity of the *Egbesu* among the youth fighters is the idea of ritual acculturation or the acquisition of membership of the group and all the rights and obligations therein through some elaborate rituals. In this sense, one can through the performance of such rituals of acculturation become Ijaw and then acquire the full rights and privileges of citizenship. A classic example of this is provided in the well-known case of the former Igbo slave – King Jaja of Opobo who rose to become a powerful Ijaw monarch in the 19th Century. Jaja underwent rituals of acculturation to become Ijaw and literally shed himself of his former "Igboness".

Chapter Three

Perception of Marginalization as Crucial Plank of the Niger Delta Struggle

Preamble

There is no gainsaying the fact that that the post-independence history of Nigeria has been pockmarked with conflict between the centre and the periphery (see, Ifeka 2000; Ujomu, 2002) and between different ethnic groups in the nation (Anugwom 2001). These conflicts have centered mainly on the issue of resources and their distribution. As Ujomu (2002: 200) posits, 'since independence in 1960, the problem of conflicts in Nigeria have centered around the experiences of the numerous individuals and groups in the country, who have been faced with oppression, marginalization, insecurity and poverty in a country so richly blessed with vast human and material resources'.

Thus, the now largely curtailed Niger Delta crisis apparently border on the feeling and perception of marginalization by the social groups in the region and to some extent identity politics. Instructively, Adedeji (1999) views marginalization as resulting from the mismanagement of the national economy and the pursuit of a development paradigm that has polarized the different social and economic groups in a given society. In this sense, poverty in the Niger Delta emanates from the pursuit of development and political strategies that instead of lessening poverty and empowering people reinforce inequality by continuing to benefit the already privileged and elite members of the society. This is equally the case in some other African nations like Togo, Benin and even the Congo where economic and political privileges have been cornered by a few elites since independence. It must have been this fact that led Harrison

(1982) to point out that the model of growth or development pursued by most Third World countries has increased inequity by channeling development opportunities to the privileged while marginalizing the less privileged.

It has been argued elsewhere (see, Anugwom, 2014; 2005; 2004 for example) that the problem of the Niger Delta region in Nigeria is tied to the issue of marginalization which is multi-faceted and severely negates the development of the region in spite of the stupendous oil wealth Nigeria produces from there. The phenomenon of marginalization as a driving force in the Niger Delta conflict in Nigeria can be captured in terms of three main currents from which the narratives on the issue have been approached. These are: an overwhelming history of socio-economic marginalization of the region in Nigeria; the decline of the derivation principle of revenue allocation; and the political domination of the area and non-performance by various governments.

History of Socio-Economic Marginalization in the Region

The marginalization angle to the Niger Delta crisis and the nexus of this marginalization to the youth involvement in conflict in the region is succinctly captured thus:

> The situation is clearly the result of the large years of internal colonialism brought to a head by oil exploitation, which degrades the environment and demoralizes the people. Local political institutions and culture have come under siege and the unemployed youths push aside the control of elders and traditional authorities that they see as ineffective against the external and internal agents that exploit the people. The disillusioned youths serve as community vanguards, which fight for control against neighboring communities over land in which new oil wells have been discovered, beginning the process of self-destruction (Alagoa, 2000: 10 cf. Oruwari, 2006).

The above observation gives a clear indication that the perception of marginalization can be seen as characterizing the advent of the region into the federal state of Nigeria right from independence. Actually, good scholars of the history of Nigeria would recall that the independence the country won from the British in 1960 would have come earlier if not for the fears of domination by ethnic majority groups expressed by minority ethnic groups especially in the Niger Delta region of Nigeria. The stridency of the ethnic minorities on the issue of likely domination by the ethnic majority groups literally forced the hands of the colonial government into setting up the popular Willink Commission to enquire into the 'Fears of Ethnic Minorities and Ways of Allaying Them' in 1957.

But contrary to the optimism of the leadership of the ethnic minorities then, the commission adopted an approach it felt would get the job done quickly and not rock the boat of the impending independence of the country. It should be remembered that the independence granted Ghana that same year (1957) made the tidying up of the Nigerian case somewhat urgent. The Willink Commission simply opted for the insertion of constitutional provisions guaranteeing the rights of minoritie[18]. Obviously, the recommendations of the commission were not enough to allay the fears of the minorities who simply adopted the practice of aligning with the political groups they feel offers the best protection of the minorities' interest in the evolving contest for political power in the emergent Nigerian state.

Minorities in the Niger Delta region just like ethnic minorities' elsewhere crave continuously for total liberation from political and economic domination by larger groups. This

---

[18] In the case of the Niger Delta region, the Willink Commission acknowledged that the terrain constituted a major problem to development in the area and thus recommended the setting up of a special agency – the Niger Delta Development Board to address the genuine development problems of the area

natural inclination of ethnic minorities has not been helped in the case of Nigeria by the long list of grievances which the oil-rich Niger Delta perceives it has endured in the Nigerian state. These overwhelming grievances of the Niger Delta which have been captured in various forms by a good number of scholars and sources include the crude oil generated pollution and environmental degradation in the region; poverty and economic want; youth unemployment; discriminatory employment practices by the oil corporations; political marginalization; socio-economic neglect etc. (see, Obi, 2008; 2007; Anugwom 2008; 2007; Omeje, 2006; Okonta and Doughlas, 2001; Ikelegbe, 2006 etc.).

These grievances have been long standing and have given rise to popular imagination in the Niger Delta region represented by the argument that the ethnic majority controlled federal government in Nigeria has literally conspired with Trans-National Oil Corporations (TNOCs) to exploit the Niger Delta by stealing their resources, damaging their environment and ensuring in the process that the indigenes hardly benefit from the billions of dollars of petroleum money generated from their environment and are neither compensated for the pollution nor the land acquired by the above outside forces in exploiting the oil in the region. The above stream of thought or reframing of the Niger Delta plight is well captured in the writings of the late Saro-Wiwa (1995); Okilo (1980); Naneen (1995); Okonta and Doughlas (2001); and Okonta (2008) among others.

A critical example of the litany of injustice to the Niger Delta region is often portrayed in the process of disempowering the people totally from control over their oil resources encapsulated in the promulgation of regulatory and compensatory laws in the oil industry by the central government in Nigeria. These laws coming from the government at the centre have literally made the Niger Delta peoples tenants in their land. While I cannot delve into a full examination of the details of these laws, their mention and a few tidbits about them may be necessary in establishing the context of marginalization in the Niger Delta struggle. The first comprehensive legal framework in this regard came with the enactment of the Petroleum Act (Decree No.51) of 1969. Other similar legislations include: The Petroleum (Drilling and Production) Regulations (Petroleum Act) of 1969 ;the Oil Pipelines Act (Decree No.31) of 1956; Land Use Decree/Act (1978); Associated Gas (Re-injection)(Act No. 99) of 1979 – the highlight of this law was its stipulation of deadline for gas flaring which it put as January 1984; another law, the 'Associated Gas Re-Injection (Continuing Flaring of Gas) Regulations of 1984' obviously took care of the inability of the industry operators to stop gas flaring (which incidentally is still on) and rather stipulated the issuance of a certificate of authorization for flaring in particular field or fields to designated firms; the 1984 law was subsequently amended in 1985 and gave terms and penalties for gas flaring as may be stipulated by the oil minister; then there is the Federal Environment Protection Agency (FEPA) (Decree. No. 58) of 1988 (subsequently amended in 1992), which established the agency and gave it the overall responsibility for protecting and managing the environment as well as advising the government on the environment. But the laws of 1969 and 1978 can be seen as the most disempowering and challenging for the people of the region.

Thus, apart from the obnoxious and alienating Petroleum Act of 1969 which ceded all petroleum resources in Nigeria to the federal government, the last nail in the coffin as it were, in estranging the Niger Delta people from their oil resources can be seen in the largely unpopular Land Use Decree/Act enacted by the military regime of Olusegun Obasanjo in 1978. In a very revealing insight, the Nigerian political scientist Kingsley Omeje captured the disempowering effects of the law on the people of the Niger Delta. Thus, 'what evidently compounds the institutional disadvantage of the oil-bearing communities and the stultification of their customary land rights is that the 1978

Act denies courts the jurisdiction to inquire into matters of compensation relating to the provisions of the Act' (Omeje, 2005b: 324).

In its bare essentials, the Act bequeaths all land onto the federal government represented by the state governors in the respective states of the federation and thus the matter of compensation becomes possible as a token since the mere ownership of the land by the government voids the claim to the land or compensation therein from the people. So the Act which serves the very ingenious purpose of government by dispossessing all Nigerians of their lands (typified by the Niger Delta plight because of the oil in the land), at the same instance takes away the control and choice of compensation from the people who in the above situation may be seen as suffering double jeopardy. While the Act applies to the whole of Nigeria, no one is deceived about the fact that the Niger Delta region suffers its negative implications more than any other geo-ethnic group. Incidentally the other areas of the country especially the land rich North of Nigeria derives some benefits from the Act in the sense that whenever government invokes the power of the Act and takes over a given portion of land from any state in the North, it is usually for development purposes i.e. building of educational institutions, roads, factories, markets, etc. but in the Niger Delta the law makes the people effectively tenants on their own land.

The Decline of the Derivation Principle of Revenue Allocation

Probably more fundamental to the Niger Delta crisis is the issue of resources allocation in Nigeria's federalism. The Niger Delta activists see politics as behind the allocation system which when the wealth of the nation was from the regions of the major ethnic groups favored a derivation principle that ensured that the region producing the larger resources gets the lion share but the principle is now largely reversed. In this reversal derivation became only a tiny component of the allocation principle (see, Anugwom, 2005). Onwuemedo (2000) captures this better by arguing that the demands of the groups and communities in the Niger Delta region are basically for socio-political conditions which would guarantee them improved living conditions, equitable revenue derivation formula and the provision of facilities that would make their lives more meaningful. Equally moving is the sentiments of a former governor in the region who has alleged ethnic majority complicity in the derivation principle decline and the use of money made from the region to develop the North of the country (see, Anugwom, 2000). This accusation may after all not be mere malice since Omeje (2006) identifies an unstable coalition of some ethnic majority elites representing the state as one party to the conflict. However, the decline of the derivation principle with the advent of oil has meant that oil-producing communities are not given the lion share of revenue from it. Given the injustice this implies as well as the massive environmental destruction associated with oil exploitation, the Niger Delta people may have felt marginalized and deprived of citizenship rights (see, Anugwom, 2014; 2004; Naanen, 1995).

One major manifestation of this fact is the often stated discontent of the people of the region with the revenue allocation or distribution system in Nigeria. The dispute or discomfort then is over what is called the derivation principle of revenue distribution (see Anugwom 2005). The derivation principle as already alluded is the regulatory framework which provides for revenue allocation in proportion to the contribution of each federating unit (state) to the federal revenue. However, this proportion which in the 1960s and early 1970s era of dependence on primary agricultural products (groundnut, cocoa, palm oil) was as high as 50% has been characterized as declining as oil gained prominence in the national economy. Thus, there is an inverse relationship (actually starting from the first regime of Olusegun Obasanjo between

1975 and 1979) between derivation proportion of revenue and contribution of oil to national revenue.

Therefore, the noted decline in the derivation principle and the introduction of the federation account system (or the so-called Distributive Pool Account – DPA) that emphasized the use of the main criteria of demographic size and need and relegated derivation to a minor criterion was seen by the Niger Delta elites as not just injustice but a manifestation of majoritarian ethnic groups' conspiracy against the people of the region (see for instance, Okilo, 1980; Saro-Wiwa, 1995; 1994; 1992; Okonta, 2008 – who introduced the salutary need to make a distinction between ethnic majority group and ethnic majority elites etc.). Quite a lot of beef has been made over the above glaring facts that one is inclined not to evoke a full discourse of the revenue contribution and sharing logic or illogic in modern Nigeria here (see, Ikein and Briggs-Anigboh, 1998 for instance for a detailed narration in this regard). However, for my concern here the sentiments of Cyril Obi (2008) would capture the essence of the grievance. Thus:

> It was also strongly felt that the principle of derivation which gave 50 per cent of revenues to the old regional governments controlled by the dominant ethnic groups was abandoned in order to enable these same groups to control the oil wealth produced from the oil minority states. Hence the struggle between the oil minorities/states of the Niger Delta and the non-oil producing ethnic majority groups/states/federal government became the object of the politics of controlling oil revenue or resource control (Obi, 2008: 11).

In spite of the foregoing, another way of looking at the decline of the derivation principle is to relate the fall in its percentage in revenue allocation to various actions of the different administrations that have been in charge of state power at the centre in Nigeria over time. In furtherance of this aim I adapt the table on regional bias in oil revenue allocation from Iyioha (2008: 3 – 4) and Iyioha and Oriakhi (2008) thus:

Table 1: Distribution of Leadership by Notable Action on Oil by Ethnic Origin of Leader

Nigerian Leader	Notable action on Oil/Revenue	Ethnic Origin/Zone
Gen. Olusegun Obasanjo (1975 – 79)	Began the reduction of the derivation component of revenue allocation. Reduced the 50 per cent oil royalties and rent (derivation) from 50 per cent to 30 per cent. Ensured the take-off of the Warri refinery	Yoruba (South West)
Alhaji Shehu Shagari (1979 – 1983)	Established the Kaduna refinery in 1980. Further reduced the share of oil royalties and rents to state of origin /derivation from 30 per cent to a miserly 2 per cent	Hausa-Fulani (North West)
Gen. Muhammadu Buhari (1984 – 85)	Reduced the oil rents and royalties further from 2 per cent to 1.5 per cent. This incidentally remains the all-time lowest point of the	Hausa-Fulani (North West)

	derivation component of national revenue allocation.	
Gen. Ibrahim Badamosi Babangida (IBB) (1985 – 1993)	Established the Oil Minerals Producing Area Development Commission (OMPADEC) in 1992. Also established the Federal Environmental Protection Agency (FEPA) in 1988. Increased the share of oil royalties and rents in the DPA from 1.5 per cent to 3 per cent	Hausa-Fulani (North Central)
Chief Ernest Shonekan (August 1993 – November 1993)	A stop-gap government; totally lacking in character or action. Took no noticeable action in anything including oil for the short period	Yoruba (South West)
Gen. Sani Abacha	Usurped power from Shonekan in a palace coup in 1993. Unleashed the severest repression ever on the Niger Delta activists. Hanged the MOSOP leader Ken Saro-Wiwa in a manner seen in	Hausa-Fulani (North West)

	most quarters as extra-judicial	
Gen. Abdulsalami Abubakar (1998 – 99)	Mid-wifed the return of democracy to Nigeria in 1999. Left the derivation component as he found it. Obviously too busy with the democratic challenge	Hausa-Fulani (North Central)
Olusegun Obasanjo (1999 – 2007)	Obasanjo's second coming but in a civilian capacity. Established the Niger Delta Development Commission (NDDC) the successor of the OMPADEC. NDDC produced the first ever Niger Delta master plan of development. Increased the derivation or oil royalties and rents from 3 per cent to 13 per cent ostensibly to enhance development of the Niger Delta and tackle ecological problems. Allowed the collapse of Nigeria's refineries	Yoruba (South-West)
Umaru Musa Yar' Ádua (2007 – 2009)	Younger brother of the more famous	Hausa-Fulani (North West)

	Shehu. Established the initial ₦50 Billion Amnesty Programme aimed at disarming the Niger Delta militants and re-skilling them for civilian life. Established the first ever Niger Delta ministry and improved budget allocation to the NDDC. Appeared unwilling to negotiate on derivation but the amnesty programme has been largely successful in bringing relative peace to the Niger Delta despite the unfortunate demise of Yar'Adua in 2009.	
Jonathan Goodluck (2009 -2015)	Continued with his predecessor's amnesty programme. Turned a good number of the erstwhile militant commanders and over-lords into overnight billionaires who lived and acted above the law.	Ijaw (South-South)

	However, did not improve the derivation component beyond 13% in spite of being a Niger Delta minority.	
Muhammadu Buhari	Another second coming in civilian capacity. Has faced challenges of peace in the Niger Delta resulting from the resurgence of militancy especially from the nascent Niger Delta Avengers (NDA). Launched the oil spill clean-up of Ogoniland based on the ground breaking UNEP (2011) Report on Ogoni land	Hausa-Fulani (North West)

Source: Adapted from Iyioha and Orakhi (2008) and Updated by Author

The above table which clearly shows the journey and politics of the derivation principle in Nigeria also sheds further light on the often taken for granted thesis of ethnic majority conspiracy or marginalization visited on the Niger Delta. As the table clearly depicts the conspiracy thesis can only be sustained on the basis of an ethnic duopoly. In this sense, the two largest ethnic groups that have controlled power at the centre since the 1970s in Nigeria are the ones that one may comfortably associate with the conspiracy thesis.

Be that as it may, it is important to note that the case of marginalization of the Niger Delta while obvious cannot be sustained in practical terms on the basis of ethnicity. Ethnicity may be considered only co-incident to marginalization. Any attempt to push the ethnic factor beyond this would amount to voiding the glaring reality of socio-economic life in Nigeria nowadays which cuts across ethno-regional divides in its negative impact but at the same time cuts a sheer clean divide between the political elites (and their economic collaborators) and the subaltern members of the Nigerian society irrespective of ethnic group or region. In other words, in spite of whatever arguments to the contrary, the socio-economic situation of the political elites in the Niger Delta is consistent in all major respects with those of their colleagues in the Hausa-Fulani North or the Yoruba South-West of Nigeria. In the same logic, the subalterns in the Hausa-Fulani or Yoruba enclaves of Nigeria share the same socio-economic fate in all major respects with their "kin" in the Niger Delta region of Nigeria. Therefore, while the ethnic majoritarian conspiracy may serve schematic convenience, it is analytically fraught with problems and is similar to a carefree reductionism that distorts reality.

Political Domination and Non-Performance by Government

Political marginalization even though manifested in the perpetual control of political power at the centre by the major ethnic groups, is made more problematic by the development dynamics, which is promoted by these major ethnic group leaders, which ends up further worsening the situation of the ethnic minorities especially in the Niger Delta region. According to the UNDP (2006: 11), 'a major concern is the region's longstanding exclusion from the mainstream of Nigeria's socio-economic and political activities. The majority of the people in the delta live on the margins'. Omeje (2006: 4) recognises this imagery among the people of the Niger Delta, "the Niger Delta minorities charge the state with deliberate marginalization and gross insensitivity to their plights, and with colluding with oil prospecting companies whose activities result in substantial devastation of the Delta environment".

It would amount to stating the obvious to argue that the problems of the Niger Delta in spite of all efforts appear largely unsolvable because of the decades of neglect and deception which various governments have adopted in viewing the problem. Thus, it was convenient at the early stages for government to adopt the attitude that the protests and activities of the oil minorities and militants were simply acts of economic sabotage and criminality which in view of threats to political stability and economic viability of the Nigerian state demanded nothing but high-handed military approach. This approach which was not helped by the military era in the governance of Nigeria was equally favoured by the political class until quite recently. Therefore the situation was given a long time to both incubate and ferment into a hydra-headed problem.

Given the dilly-dallying and obtuse refusal of various governments in Nigeria to deal effectively with the problem; the conflict eventually transformed in the 2000s into what is now also popularly known as the 'resource control' struggle. However, the popularity of the concept of resource control has much to do with the attempt of the decadent political elites from the region to hijack the struggle and bleed it for political gains. While this aim of the political class worked in some cases as typified in the popular clamor for the release of a former governor of Bayelsa state found guilty of corruption while in power and the ascension of a Niger Delta indigene to the office of Vice President of Nigeria (and later, President), it equally backfired in other cases and as shown in the metamorphosis of Asari-Dokubo and Ateke Tom [19] which often complicated matters in the feeble efforts of the government at peace building

---

[19] From errand boys and enforcers for political godfathers in Rivers state to big time militant leaders and war lords

in the region. Therefore, beside the convenient coincidence in aims between the political elites (represented by the state governors in the region; undoubtedly motivated also by the boost in state revenue allocation from the Distributable Pool Account (DPA) that a successful struggle would entail) and the ordinary people and civil society organizations in the region which the resource control campaign manifested, it sought mainly to achieve three well-articulated and related objectives viz.:

- Right to self-determination by the people of the region to be characterized primarily by their control of the natural resources in the area
- Adequate compensation for the accumulated environmental/ecological damage visited on the region by decades of oil exploitation. The compensation would broadly cover damages inflicted by pollution; environmental degradation; and the resulting loss of livelihood by the people of the region
- The overriding justification of actions from the different elements in the Niger Delta on the basis of the injustice in the control of the oil from the region by a federal government controlled by elites from the ethnic majority groups. Therefore, the granting of unconditional political amnesty to the youth militants and other resource control activists in the region.

Okonta (2008) provides commendable insight into the way the long standing neglect of the Niger Delta people by the government and its reaction to agitations to address genuine concerns of the various groups in the region helped transform the struggle into a violent one. Thus, he traces the frustration and anger of the Ogoni elites and by implication other oil bearing communities in the Niger Delta to the fact that they saw the revenues from oil taken from their land go to elites from the major ethnic groups to the detriment of Ogoni elites who felt sidelined. But besides the above, he argues that the utilization of

66

the hitherto burgeoning oil revenues in cities while most Ogoni lived in the rural areas where the oil boom largesse did not reach was another source of frustration for the ordinary Ogoni. For him, the interaction between the above elite anger and rural deprivation exploded into militant Ogoni nationalism in the 1990s.

However, the above contentions as revealing as they are can easily be perceived as freezing history or slanting it to favor Niger Delta separatism which breeds an imagery that casts the people of the region as totally inculpable in the problem there. In this case while it explains the coincidence between the perception of marginalization by the Ogoni elite and rural neglect which crystallized into the Ogoni ethnic nationalism in the early 1990s, the role of the Ogoni and Niger Delta elites in the late 1990s and onwards made them more or less collaborators with political elites in other parts of Nigeria. In fact, in a report in 2009, another Niger Delta activist Ann Kio Briggs lambasted the Niger Delta governors for wasting enormous resources allocated to the region and as having failed their people and thus have no right to remain in power (Daily Trust, 2009).

In spite of whatever may be the merit of the above utterances credited to Briggs, the elongation of historical facts or their slanting which Okonta inadvertently privileges may sustain the smokescreen which so far has protected Niger Delta political elites from accounting for whatever little they have received from the federation account. Thus, if the accounts in the Daily Trust newspaper report are accurate what the Niger Delta region (in this case the Southsouth zone made up of Bayelsa, Rivers, Delta, Edo, Akwa Ibom and Cross River States) received from the federation account in 2008 (N827billion) is higher than those of the other regions in the country combined. Incidentally the Southeastern zone with two oil producing states (Imo and Abia) received the least (N176billion) for the same year.

Another critical fact of the oil exploitation in the Niger Delta of Nigeria and the conflicts around it which is often overlooked is the role of international capital and external forces who are collaborators with different levels of government in it. The high stakes in the oil industry in Nigeria positions the militants and local communities against the forces of the national government and political elites in Nigeria who are in alliance with international capitalist's interests represented most physically by the oil corporations. Omeje (2006) in a very insightful contribution shows how the local oil bearing communities are more or less victims in this arrangement (see also Okonta, 2008 for a version of this thinking in relation to the Ogoni ethnic group in the Niger Delta). However, Obi (2008: 8) has argued,

> While most of the attention is often placed on local actors: the state/political elites, militia groups/warlords, and weak and inept bureaucracies, very little attention is paid to the role of external and transnational actors and the lack of transparency that shrouds the extent of their involvement in these conflicts. Such external actors include private security organizations, mercenaries, international traders and companies, arms suppliers, and extra-African powers pursuing strategic and economic interests in the continent.

What emanates from the discourse so far in this chapter is the realization of the overwhelming feeling of injustice and exclusion which generates the conflict in the Niger Delta region. These are captured essentially in local parlance in the extensive use of the notion of marginalization. Marginalization is an idiom for inequity in resource allocation; environmental degradation; and ethnic minority exploitation of diverse forms in Nigeria. Therefore, the ethnic plank on which Okonta (2008) has tried an admirable analysis of the Ogoni project in contemporary Nigeria should be considered instructive to an extent in unraveling the driving force behind youth involvement in the

Niger Delta conflict. It actually affirms that the ethnic factor (whether instrumentalised or exploited) which in the case of the Niger Delta region positions ethnic minorities at the receiving end of ethnic majority elites injustice as well as the framing of separatism as natural, beneficial and the logical route to dissociation of marginalization makes participation by all segments of the society especially the youth alluring. However, the ethnicity logic is limited in explaining the Niger Delta case in its entirety since there is evidence of massive rentier elite collaboration crisscrossing all ethnic groups in Nigeria since the democratic era in 1999.

Therefore, the subaltern Niger Delta citizens share more in common in privileges and access to resources with subalterns in other areas of the country than with Niger Delta elites. In other words, the utility of the ethnic tool should be anchored on the understanding that ethnic majority elites much like their ilks in the minority areas exploit both state power and popular imagery of their respective groups for their own selfish purposes. The above is however not really new since a similar phenomenon has been detected in the Congo case where ethnic solidarity has made most families send their children to fight for militia groups claiming to fight for the interests of their ethnic group (see, Beneduce et al, 2006). So the gospel of ethnic majoritarian conspiracy and acute marginalization are instrumentally used to sustain not just youth involvement but also the support of the ethnic minorities in the Niger Delta region.

Overview of Recent Regulatory Framework of the Oil Industry in Nigeria

Even though I have briefly examined some of the critical elements of the regulatory environment of oil in the preceding section, it is in order to throw further light on this especially in the bid to capture more recent developments. As obvious from the foregoing, one way of summarizing the above grievances and dissatisfaction of the oil producing communities in Nigeria in general is that these communities are dissatisfied with the entire regulatory framework which governs oil exploitation in the country. It is this framework which apart from critically determining who gets what from the oil in the country also sets limits to both expectations and demands from the parties involved. One crucial shortfall of the regulatory framework until very recently was the inability to see the oil bearing communities as fit for any concrete benefits beyond the tokenism of corporate social responsibility and menial jobs. It could be argued that the watershed which the efforts towards an enactment of a radical regulatory framework which defines the communities as *bona fide* owners or partners in the exploitation of petroleum resources started during the government of the late Umaru Yar'Adua and can be attributed to the resilience of the youth militants from the Niger Delta who have kept the problems of the region consistently on the national consciousness and front burner of development discourse in the country for decades.

But the first comprehensive legal framework was the Petroleum Act (Decree No.51) of 1969 which was followed by others especially the equally decisive Land Use Decree/Act of 1978. Without doubt there have been major developments in the regulatory environment of the oil industry in Nigeria since the 1990s[20]. One outcome of the efforts at changing the regulation was the enactment of The Nigerian Oil and Gas Industry Local Content Development Act (2010) which seeks to put more of the upstream sector of the oil industry in the hands of Nigerians. So, it provides that Nigerian independent operators shall be given first consideration in the awards of oil blocks; oil fields

---

[20] One is not forgetting the other influential regulations like the Petroleum Profits Tax (PPT) Act and the Deep Offshore and Inland Basin Production Sharing Contracts Act both of which have governed revenue generation and sharing in joint ventures in the country. Also worth mentioning is the influential Nigerian Extractive Industries Transparency Initiative (NEITI) Act which actually informs the provisions of the PIB on transparency.

and oil lifting licenses etc. in the oil and gas industry in Nigeria. This law is one of the outcomes of the debates generated by the activism of the Niger Delta youth regarding the inequity of the oil exploitation *status quo* for decades.

In addition to the foregoing, there is also the existence of the National Oil Spill Detection and Response Agency (NOSDRA) which was established through a 2006 Act of Parliament in Nigeria. The main function of this agency is to detect oil spills and engender actions to address spills and stop further spills in the Nigerian environment especially in the oil producing areas. However, during a recent symposium in 2016 the agency bemoaned the fact that the regulation establishing it does not give it the power to sanction or really criminalize acts of oil spillage by groups and organizations in Nigeria. It therefore seeks the modification of the law to empower it to take actions against oil spillers without which it believes oil spillage eradication would be far-fetched in Nigeria. In view of the above, the NOSDRA despite the enthusiasm of its members and even some neutral watchers of the oil industry has been more or less powerless in taking actions at eradication of oil spillage. Thus, while it rightly detects spills, it cannot take action against those responsible even when it occurs as a result of the flagrant disregard for safe environmental practices.

Probably, the most cogent of the desired changes which bears direct relevance to the quest of the youth militants and the conflict in the oil producing areas is the Nigeria Petroleum Industry Bill (PIB). The Bill has been seen by informed observers as a very ambitious attempt to comprehensively reform or overhaul the oil and gas sector in the country (see, Okhomina, 2010; Heller, 2010). In fact, Heller (2010: 1) argues, 'Nigeria's Petroleum Industry Bill (PIB) represents an ambitious attempt to implement much needed reform to the structure, governance, and fiscal rules of the country's oil industry, which has been beset for years by corruption and inefficiency'. However, in characterising the Bill, the government oil monopoly, the NNPC sees it as 'an Act to establish the legal and regulatory framework, institutions and regulatory authorities for the Nigerian petroleum industry, to establish guidelines for the operation of the upstream and downstream sectors and for purposes connected with the same' (NNPC, 2010: 1).

The Bill seeks to address the two main Achilles heels of the exploitation of petroleum resources in Nigeria which have fed into the widespread and often violent agitations in the oil producing areas. These are the failure of the government (through its agencies especially the NNPC) and the TNOCs to evolve adequate mechanisms through the years for ensuring the protection of the social and physical environment in the oil producing areas and for ensuring that the oil bearing or producing communities benefit in some predictable and significant ways from oil exploitation. In essence, the Bill proposes to hold the government accountable for promoting community development and ensuring that damage to communities where oil is exploited is minimal. Also, companies are required to develop and submit environmental quality management plans to the government and to pay a sum to a federal inspectorate outfit (to be established by the Bill) for site rehabilitation or environmental correction. The PIB in summary aims at transforming the oil industry into an engine of sustainable development in Nigeria; enhancing governance; and the elimination of toxic social and environmental impacts on the oil bearing communities.

It is however imperative to make the point that the problem goes beyond the law but necessarily includes the enforcement of the regulations in ways that guarantee the spirit of the laws and safeguard the environment. Given a high corruption level, the laws in different spheres of public life in Nigeria are only for those without the means to circumvent them. It is in this regard, that the policing of the parties especially the TNOCs and the agents and agencies of the state in Nigeria to ensure that the laws regarding the exploitation of oil resources especially as they pertain to the oil bearing communities and environmental responsibility are kept is critical. Particularly, the Bill has been criticized as falling short of creating tangible measures for achieving the laudable goals of limiting environmental damage and holding companies operating in the oil sector totally responsible for community development initiatives that should be ideally derived in collaboration with the communities (see, Heller, 2010; Okhomina, 2010 for more on these shortcomings).

Moreover, one really wonders if the Bill represents the 'know it all and take care of it all phenomenon' that it is often seen as among government circles. Thus, 'the Bill is a massive and imperfect piece of legislation, and the debate around it has been contentious and multi-faceted' (Heller, 2010: 1). Nothing acutely validates the above assertion made about five years ago more than the fact that six years down the line (2016) the PIB as salutary as it seems in most major respects is yet to be passed into law by the federal legislature. As a matter of fact, there are increasing suspicions among the petroleum industry watchers in Nigeria that the Bill has largely been emasculated of its original provisions especially in reference to the duties and obligations of the TNOCs over the past few years of rancor and unproductive debates in the National Assembly.

Chapter Four

What The Theories Tell Us

Preamble

Quite a good number of studies have established a relationship between a country's reliance on natural resources endowment and both the likelihood of conflict and the duration of such conflict (see, Collier and Hoeffler, 2001; Soysa, 2000; Elbadawi and Sambani, 2002; Auty, 2003). There is therefore, a robust body of theory on the issue of conflict, resource conflict and youth conflict in Africa. The theories or explanations which scholars have utilized in capturing the reality of conflict especially those related to natural resources have been challenged incidentally by both the frequency of these conflicts and their diverse forms in different parts of Africa. Generally, some make-shift division between political conflicts and resource conflicts may be attempted; however such efforts are voided by a realization that in Africa as much the scenario elsewhere in the world social conflicts are usually anchored on multiple factors.

In other words, it may be tenuous to make a strict separation between political or ethnic conflicts and economic or resource conflicts since the pursuit of economic goals are often coincidental or co-terminous with political goals for any given group. Therefore, while one may see a triggering factor of the conflict in the political or economic realm, the dynamics of conflict between groups in modern society usually tend towards a holistic rejection, resistance to or negotiation of the *status quo ante*. In this sense, conflicts have a dynamism that eludes easy separation into neat and impermeable categories in modern society. In fact, as the case of states in Africa has shown, conflict which originates from a given factor may in effect represent a total rejection of the existing socio-political and economic order.

In view of the above, a strong leaning towards any particular theory may be seen as not always advisable in explaining different social conflicts in Africa. However, the reliability of theoretical explanations has improved in cases where they have addressed a given conflict as a prototype of conflicts in Africa. While this has not helped overcome the universally acknowledged limits of theories in explaining all observable phenomena, it has also limited the validity of such explanations since they may become unhelpful in other similar contexts. Hence, theories of conflict in post-colonial African societies have focused on general characteristics or attributes of these societies and states that trigger or predispose them to conflict especially in the resource allocation or distribution process. Along the above traditions, this chapter tries a critical review of the myriad theories that have been invoked by scholars through the years in explaining resource related conflicts in Africa in general.

The Usual Suspects: Patrimonialism; Neo-Patrimonialism and Triple Alliance

Patrimonialism

One of the most popular explanations of the Niger Delta crisis and in fact development dilemma generally in Nigeria is the patrimonial state framework. In this overtly political science approach, social conflict, instability and underdevelopment can all be linked to the patrimonial nature of the modern Nigerian state. Therefore, while retaining the outward characteristics of institutionalized administrative states, the state in reality operates along a patron-client network and trajectories embedded in historical patterns of authority and social solidarity (see, Grugel, 2002). Hence, the state while appropriating the superficial garb of modernity is in reality also a counter-imagery of modernism since it blurs the distinction between private and public resources and even between the secular and the sacred.

In this case, the resources of the state and access to them are channeled on a patron-client network in a typical patrimonial mode which is both intricate and reinforcing. Predictably, the scenario makes the political elites dispensers of both power and resources and in the process creates the perception of public office as equally personal domains of appropriation. Joseph (1987) has done a good job of capturing this dynamics in his influential notion of 'prebendalism' in Nigeria. According to him, state offices in Nigeria are regarded as 'prebends' that can be easily appropriated by office holders for personal goals; a mentality and perception which he sees as the major bulwark against democracy in modern Nigeria.

Even though a concept commonly invoked these days, patrimonialism owes its ascendancy in intellectual discourse to its usage by Weber (1947) to describe a scenario where the administrative apparatus is appointed by and totally responsible to the top leader. Weber went on to compare patrimonialism with the rational-legal system and in typical Weberian thought saw the later as superior and better-attuned to the development of society. In most of Africa and other parts of the developing world, a patrimonial system emerges in which government offices and public positions are conceived as income (profit) generating opportunities for the occupants and their cronies or relations.

The unwavering irony is that in these countries including Nigeria even though there is an expansive superstructure of rational-legal administration in line with that promoted by Weber, government business and public administration are conducted generally on patrimonial basis. In other words, the rational-legal frameworks are only there for appearance and in fulfilment of the books while policy implementation and access to resources depend on a network of patrons, personal retainers and their dependents/cronies. Therefore, the above system which characterises governance (in Nigeria) can be made culpable for the development problems not only in the oil-producing Niger Delta but the entire country as well.

Neo-Patrimonialism

The outmoding of patrimonialism at the immediate aftermath of colonialism in a lot of African nations gave rise to neo-patrimonialism which is still a continuation of the clientele type of politics and economic distribution which reinforces inequality while perpetuating the reign of primordialism. Thus, neo-patrimonialism encourages a vertical distribution of both resources and access to valuable positions in the society often anchored on a strong network built around a powerful individual, group or even political party. It works on the basis of clientelism or the patron-client network model of politics which can be found not only in Africa but even in other developing nations of the world. The notion of clientelism owes its origin to the social sciences especially sociology and anthropology where Schmidt et al (1997) show, it was used to describe hierarchical social relations in predominantly peasant societies.

However, clientelism nowadays is the favoured route of operations especially in what can be called insecure political and economic settings in which it is seen as critical to the survival of both patrons and clients. In Nigerian parlance it is captured in the form of the inevitability of the politics of survival expressed on the street level with the metaphor – if you rub my back, I will rub your back. A form of reciprocity which incidentally undermines both the rules of formality and legality in political and business conduct. In the relationship, the patron is ideally the one who calls the shots and dispenses socio-political favours but is equally dependent on the client for return favours especially in terms of support for political office. As Thomson (2004: 127) argues, patronage entails the centralization of power on an "individual to whom all within the system owe their positions". In typical cases, there is a network of patrons and clients though in authoritarian or dictatorial regimes, a single individual wields ultimate power and oils the whole network.

But critically important is that what anybody gets depends on the whims of the ultimate patron and is classically a form of "exchange relations between unequals" (Boas, 2001: 700). In the developing world, neo-patrimonialism or what Erdman and Engel (2006) label modern patrimonialism breeds development maladies since it enables a process through which patronage politics or what has been called prebendal politics in the case of Nigeria (see, Joseph, 1987) supplant the legal-rational apparatus. Therefore, for a lot of people, the ineffectual utilization of huge oil resources for over five decades in Nigeria as well as the deplorable situation of the oil-bearing communities can be attributed to a persistent regime of neo-patrimonialism in governance that has characterised both military and civilian leadership in Nigeria since independence.

Bratton and van de Walle (1998) present what can be seen as one of the most popular explanations of the state and conflict in Africa in the notion of neo-patrimonialism. The notion which grew out of and is consistent in major respects with the patrimonial theory is anchored on the idea that the processes of leadership and governance in Africa are personalized and thus function through patronage rather than some overriding instrumental values as encapsulated in law or ideology. In such a situation where personal and patrimonial networks become the routes towards accessing power and resources, violence easily erupts from those who are either excluded or marginal to the process. In other words, the state in this case ultimately generates conflict. Allen (1995) has captured the kernel of the argument by postulating what he labels "spoils politics" in which self-enrichment and utilization of power for material aggrandizement become crucial realities. In this situation, the state approaches the mode of the Bayart et al (1999) notion of a criminalized state.

The Triple Alliance or Commercial Triangle Notion

Equally interesting an explanation which is anchored on a coterminous goal or interest between the domestic political elites and international capital is the triple alliance or commercial triangle notion. In this case, the theory (Turner, 1978) sees the dominant class forces in Nigeria as comprising a nexus made up of international capital, local Nigerian associates or comprador elites, and state/its officials. These three groups make up the hegemonic force behind the oil industry and strive to advance the interests of international capital and in the process assuage their own accumulative tendencies. In other words, this theory (see Turner, 1978 for instance) sees the dominant class forces in Nigeria as comprising a nexus made up of international capital, local Nigerian associates or comprador elites, and the state/its officials.

In fact, in another analysis, Omeje (2006: 2) argues that this theoretical viewpoint,

> depicts the host state in the global south as a captured state compelled to advance and protect the interests of international capital which in the Nigerian situation not only include oil investments, but also extends to the economic and political conditionalities of the neo-liberal economic reforms imposed by the World Bank and International Monetary Fund.

Apparently, the above hegemonic force is opposed to civil society which adopts a counter-narrative and discourse and hence the emergence of conflict.

Going Economic: Resource Curse; Environmental Scarcities; Grievance versus Greed

Resource Curse

The resource curse perspective has its roots in the discipline of economics (see, Sachs and Warner 2001; van Wijnbergen, 1984; Torvik, 2001). The basic premise of the perspective is that natural resources endowment alone does not automatically mean development since cases abound to show that some areas that are not well endowed resource wise have achieved more development than others better endowed. But more crucial for us here is that the perspective posits that such rich resources have often been the harbinger of conflicts and other anti-development phenomena. The now popular resource curse thesis is actually framed in a counter-intuitive logic and argues simply that not only may resource-rich countries fail to benefit from a favourable endowment; they may in reality perform worse than less well-endowed countries (Auty, 1993). Thus, 'a growing body of evidence suggests that a favourable natural resource endowment may be less beneficial to countries at low- and mid-income levels of development than the conventional wisdom might suppose'(Auty, 1993: 1).

The above contention is supported by the developing countries' postwar industrialization efforts and the performance of the mineral-rich developing countries since 1960s according to Auty (1993). Although Auty's insightful study focused essentially on the oil economies of South America like Bolivia, Peru and Chile, its findings especially in terms of the negative influence of internal economic and environmental factors is seen as telling for African oil economies (Nigeria, Angola, Gabon, Libya, Algeria, Egypt, Equatorial Guinea, Tunisia, Sudan, Rep. of Congo – Brazzaville, and lately Ghana, Cameroon and Chad) especially for Nigeria [21] where the net impact of oil on development has remained consistently low.

Nankani (1979) has earlier demonstrated that the mineral economies'economic growth and social welfare are inferior to those of the non-mineral economies at similar levels of development. Perhaps, a good way of exploring this contention would be to compare the economic growth of non-oil economies with that of Nigeria with its stupendous mineral endowment. A comparison of Nigeria's real growth in trade and export for 2007 with that of other African oil economies (Gabon and Angola) and those of non-oil economies like Ghana (significantly non-oil producing by 2007), Kenya and South Africa would be thus:

Table 2: Distribution of Country by Real Growth (Trade and Export) in 2007

Country	Real Growth (trade) 2007	Real Growth (Export) 2007
Angola	18.4	21.9
Ghana	7.3	4.7
South Africa	7.2	4.1
Gabon	7.5	4.1
Nigeria	5.0	2.1
Kenya	6.6	6.1

Source: Adapted from World Bank: World Trade Indicators 2008

While the above table of economic indicators may be fraught with a lot of inconclusive evidence since growth is essentially

---

[21] Nigeria falls squarely into the definition of a mineral economy. Auty (1993) defines the mineral economies as those developing countries that generate at least 8 per cent of their GDP and 40 per cent of their export earnings from the mineral sector. In this sense, with a mono-economy dependent on oil proceeds for both GDP and export earnings Nigeria is maximally and archetypically a mineral economy.

only one component of development though a very important one, the comparison of Nigeria with another oil economy like Angola tells a more vivid story. In this case, Angola's growth in three years (2006 to 2008) consequent upon the prominence of oil in its economy raises questions about the Nigerian development malaise. But back to the Auty contention, the table shows that such non-oil economies as at 2007 like Ghana, Kenya and South Africa outperformed Nigeria. While South Africa with its significant level of local industrialization may be no surprise, the case of Kenya and Ghana tells the Nigerian story better than any other narrative.

According to Auty (1993) the root causes of mineral economies underperformance in relation to other developing countries can be attributed to three factors viz. the mining sector's production function (i.e. ratio of capital to labour); domestic linkages; and deployment of mineral rents. There is need to properly understand the above logic and the implications for development in a mineral economy like Nigeria. In the first cause is the strong capital intensive nature of minerals which means an over-reliance on international or foreign capital and employment of a small fraction (in comparison to its share of GDP) of the national work force. Basically as the ownership structure of the Nigerian oil industry shows, the dominance of foreign capital in the guise of the TNOCs is overwhelming. In fact, Omeje's (2006) notion of high stakes derive essentially from the huge international capital involvement in Nigeria's oil industry and the nexus of interest between this and domestic rent-seekers.

The second cause is that of low domestic linkages in which case there is low revenue retention because of the need to service foreign capital investments. Moreover, the role of international capital makes the sector display enclave tendencies since it yields minimal local production linkages. But more damning from Auty's root causes perspective is the existence of substantial rents i.e. revenues in excess of production costs and normal returns to capital which when captured by the government can destabilize the economy (Auty, 1993). A good number of scholars (see, Krugman 1987; Gelb, 1988; Auty and Warhurst 1991; Corden and Neary, 1982) including Auty have seen the above reality in terms of the "Dutch Disease" notion. In effect,

> The imprudent domestic absorption of mining sector rents is capable of rendering much agricultural and manufacturing activity internationally uncompetitive. This occurs through a process known as "Dutch disease". It results from a strengthening (appreciation) of the exchange rate as a consequence of the over-rapid inflow of mineral rates into the domestic economy (Auty, 1993: 3 and 5).

It is only simple to imagine as the study of Krugman (1987) showed that Nigeria suffered this syndrome during the 1979 – 81 world oil boom and is currently suffering from it since the oil glut from 2015. The downward spiral in oil prices from a princely over $150 a barrel to current below $40 a barrel (January - March 2016) has put Nigeria's economy in comatose. Incidentally, employment has not just contracted within the oil industry in the country but there has been lay-offs as the TNOCs struggle to remain afloat.

Be that as it may, a glaring shortcoming of the resource curse thesis has been unraveled by Obi (2008) who contends that the approach does not capture the complex dimensions of the politics and international linkages that underpin violent conflicts in resource-rich African countries and does not also explain why wars break out in the resource poor countries. As a matter of fact, the endless conflagration in such resource poor countries in Africa like Ethiopia and Somalia lends credence to the above argument by Obi. Insightful as it is, the resource curse notion is incidentally not always valid. Thus, some countries with abundant natural resources do indeed perform better. In fact, Stiglitz (2004) captures this with a comparison between Nigeria

84

and Indonesia, both with oil wealth. However, Indonesia's per capita income is four times that of Nigeria.

Moreover, the resource curse argument in typical economics argument underplays the interplay of social forces in the society that determine both the exploitation and benefits of resources. Another ostensible drawback of the resource curse thesis is perhaps provided by the case of Angola where economic growth has accentuated due to the resources in the country. However, the fact of recent growth in the Angolan economy has not made it any less a fragile state and the state of poverty in the country still underlines the problem of inequity in wealth distribution. However, in comparison with Nigeria, Angola seems to manifest a more prudent use and management of oil resources (see table below). All the same, the Angola case also in some ways further lend credence to the resource curse assumption that mere resource endowment does not automatically translate to economic growth and development.

Table 3: GDP Comparison between Nigeria and Angola (A)

Country	Real GDP Growth	
	2007	2008
Nigeria*	6.3%	9.0%
Angola**	19%	11.5%

Sources: *Nigeria's Presidential Economic Intelligence Unit (EIU) reported in Business Day (2009)" Nigeria's Growth slides to 2.7% in 2009 – EIU".www.businessdayonline.com/index.php (Accessed: 10th October 2009). **Angola's Growth from "The African Economic Outlook 2008: The Pulse of Africa", from the OECD

In spite of the foregoing table, a more realistic GDP growth rate outlook is derived from the IMF thus:

Table 4: GDP Comparison between Nigeria and Angola
(B)

Year	Nigeria	Angola
2007	7%	20.3%
2008	6%	13.2%
2009	2.9%	0.2%*
2010	5.0%	9.3%

Source: IMF World Economic Outlook – www.imf.org/external/pubs/ft/weo/2009/02 * The World Bank and the Angolan government puts the GDP growth for 2009 at 10 – 11% (worldBank.org/WBsite/external/countries/Africaext/Angolaextn/0) (Accessed: 13th October 2009).

The comparison between Nigeria and Angola is not much different from the above even when GDP per capita is used. Thus:

Table 5: Comparison of GDP per Capita – Nigeria and Angola

Country	1996 - 2000	2001 - 2005	2006 - 2010	2011 – 2015
Angola	5,053.7	5,531.8	5,900.5	NA
Nigeria	2,514.1	2,739.9	2,979.8	3,203.3

Source: www.data.worldbank.org/indicator/NY.GDP.PCAP.CD
[Accessed: March 8, 2016]

In what seems like a re-interrogation of the resource curse assumption regarding the nexus between natural resources endowment and conflict, Michael Ross (2003) raises the critical question: do different types of resources have different effects on conflict? In answer to this, he shows that of all major types of natural resources, diamonds and drugs are most strongly associated with conflicts that occurred between 1990 and 2000. But perhaps more insightful is his contention that three characteristics of natural resources 'their lootability, their obstructability, and their illegality – are likely to influence civil wars' (Ross, 2003: 47).

For Ross, first, resources have sharply different effects in separatist conflict in comparison to non-separatist conflict. Second, he contends also that the impact of any given type of resource depends on whether it is 'lootable' or not and finally that 'lootable' resources like diamonds and drugs are more likely to ignite non-separatist conflicts. But for me, his important contention is that, 'unlootable resources –like oil, natural gas, and deep-shaft minerals – tend to produce separatist conflicts, but seldom influence nonseparatist conflicts. In sum, lootable resources negatively affect nonseparatist conflicts and unlootable resources negatively affect separatist conflicts' (Ross, 2003: 47 – 8).

The above contribution of Ross is really interesting in the bid to arrive at an explanation of the Nigerian oil conflict. In this sense, given that oil can hardly be seen in terms of two of the above three characteristics (it is only obstructable given the use of long pipelines and massive drilling platforms and refineries) and should be expected as a non-lootable resource to negatively affect separatist conflicts (the oil war in Nigeria had an undeniable separatist undertone). In other words, unlootable resources like oil are more likely to cause separatist conflicts than lootable resources like diamond.

Environmental Scarcities

One other perspective in the extant literature is the contention that environmental degradation which has produced scarcities in natural resources fuels civil conflict within poor states (Homer-Dixon, 1991; 1995). This thinking generally is often captured in terms of the notion of "ecoviolence" or the over-arching effect of ecological and environmental problems on conflict. However, while this approach has sometimes been represented as arguing that environmental scarcities induce war

87

or conflict, the views of Homer-Dixon (1995) is simply that environmental degradation generates scarcity which in turn produces conflict as a result of struggle for access and control over what is left. The scarcity related conflict occurs through, first, resource scarcity driving elites to capture resources and thus marginalizing powerless groups. Perhaps, this is well captured in the idea that, 'resource capture occurs when the degradation and depletion of renewable resources interact with population growth to encourage powerful groups within society to shift resource distribution in their favour' (Homer-Dixon, 1999: 177).

Also, Homer-Dixon envisages a second way in what he calls the "ingenuity gap" which simply posits that poor countries are confronted with fast moving and interacting environmental scarcities which overwhelm efforts towards producing constructive change which can affect ability to deliver reform. For him, these can generate a self-enforcing spiral of violence, institutional dysfunction and social fragmentation in the society. The sum of the Homer-Dixon perspective is that poor countries remain poor and suffer from conflict because resource scarcity erodes or prevents socio-economic innovation or reform. The above situation is seen as self-reinforcing and resembles a vicious cycle.

The interesting thing about the eco-violence or environmental scarcity argument is that it stands as a formidable opposition to the resource curse thesis. However, it equally suffers some of the weaknesses of the resource curse thesis especially in terms of not caring too much about the social relations of resource exploitation; the role of international capital and the fact that the states in question are neither monolithic wholes nor cut-off totally from the global economic system. Moreover, as the case of the Niger Delta of Nigeria shows while environmental degradation may be a strong factor in conflict (see Anugwom, 2007), groups often engage in the struggle for resources or conflict over resources long before the point of scarcity is perceived. Therefore, while the eco-violence perspective may well be a reliable explanation elsewhere in Africa, its explanatory power in the Niger Delta crisis seems severely limited.

Grievance versus Greed

In seeking amelioration of the complex Niger Delta oil conflict, it may well be advisable to take note of the economic gain dimension to the conflict. In this regard, Collier (2000) argues that economic agenda appear central to understanding why civil wars or conflicts start. For him therefore, if economic agenda drive conflicts, then it is likely that some groups benefitting from conflict would have an interest in both initiating and sustaining it. In the sociological frame, these social groups or elements are those with vested interest in the continuation or persistence of conflict. In the Niger Delta case, while the visible operators of the oil joint ventures i.e. the TNOCs and their allied firms and the Nigerian government through the NNPC would see the cessation of the conflict which has undermined the proceedings from oil and gulped resources that could have been employed elsewhere as desirable, the case might be different with regards to the shadow operators in the region. These shadow operators typified by the oil bunkering mafia and gun runners have a stake in the continuation of the conflict since insecurity readily provides cover for their shadow businesses.

The Social Mix: Bottom-up and Top-down; Relative Deprivation

Relative Deprivation:

One way of credibly explaining ethno-nationalism especially in heterogeneous societies like Nigeria is to posit the sociological notion of relative deprivation. In this sense, restiveness and dissatisfaction over resource allocation derives from a rational comparison of a group's shares and benefits with those of significant others. In this process of comparison a negative balance between both perceived contribution and benefit or between the group's share and that of another group seen as contributing same or less breed psychological dissonance which easily generates conflict. Deprivation apart from being instructive in studying individual action has been found useful in explaining the emergence and persistence of social movements (see, Igbo and Anugwom, 2002). In this sense, a group that feels short-changed in relation to others in the same society may engage in actions to expunge or address this deprivation. Therefore the deprivation theory contends that people who feel deprived of some good or resources are more likely than others to engage in political/social actions to address the deprivation.

The allure of the classical deprivation theory of classical sociology in explaining the Niger Delta crisis derives from the relative nature of the debilitating socio-economic conditions in the region. The region is globally one of the poorest oil bearing areas (see, UNDP, 2006); the region is one of the poorest in the country; and social infrastructure development in the region is one of the lowest in Nigeria. Perhaps, Afeikhena (2005: 15) utilizing the OPEC Factsheet in a recent World Bank Report captures the logic properly by stating,

> 'about 80 per cent of Nigeria's oil and natural gas revenues accrue to one per cent of the country's population. The other 99 per cent of the population receive the remaining 20 per cent of the oil and gas revenues leaving Nigeria with the lowest per capita oil export earning put at $212 (N28, 408) per person in 2004'.

The above sentiment which is valid today (if not more so, given a recessionary economy) as it was in 2005 is consistent with the UNDP (2006) report which describes the socio-economic condition of the Niger Delta region as extremely poor and unsustainable and characterizes the region as a development paradox given the tremendous oil wealth it generates and the penury under which its inhabitants live.

The relative deprivation felt by the people of the Niger Delta may not really be in terms of comparing their individual lot with that of significant others but either in comparison of development in the region and that in other areas especially the North (development infrastructure like roads, bridges, pipe-borne water, federal government presence in terms of establishment of agencies and institutions etc.). It is also generally seen in popular discourse as manifested in the control and access to the oil resources especially in terms of allocation of oil prospecting licenses, oil blocks; the leadership of the Nigerian National Petroleum Corporation (NNPC) and general participation of the people of the region in the downstream petroleum sector in the country..

However the explanatory power of this orientation is often short-circuited by the fact that it fails to explain why relative deprivation does not generate social action in all groups. Thus, it does not pose a reliable direct relationship between deprivation and socio-political consciousness. In a manner of speaking, it really tells only one half of the story.

Bottom-Up Perspective

In an interesting piece on conflict, David Keen (2000) made a distinction between 'bottom-up' and 'top-down' violence. In this case, the latter is the violence mobilized by political leaders and entrepreneurs for economic or political reasons in which case coercion becomes a way of recruiting fighters or soldiers for this violence. On the other hand, the "bottom-up" violence is violence actively embraced by a variety of ordinary people as solution to problems of their own. But more insightful than the above mere distinction is his argument that, 'in order to move toward more lasting solutions for the problem of mass violence, we need to understand and acknowledge that for significant groups this violence represents not a problem but a solution' (Keen, 2000: 25). In relation to the Niger Delta conflict, one may rightly see the conflict as largely a 'bottom-up' type of violence though the initial articulation of the problem by Saro-Wiwa and his cohorts may not really be typical bottom-up and there is undoubtedly good reasons to suspect the involvement of elite elements to an extent in it till date. However, the main interest of Keen's idea is in terms of the determination of the extent to which the perception of violence as a solution can be seen as a factor in the sustenance of the Niger Delta conflict.

Chapter Five

Debate with Religion: The Religious Cocktail of Occult, Witchcraft and Sorcery

Defining Religion

As any social scientist and particularly scholars of religion in general would easily concede the definition of religion generally is inherently controversial. The controversy is associated mainly with what religion implies in real terms or the empirical referents of the concept of religion especially from a global or cross-cultural perspective. Melford Spiro contends that,

> an examination of the definitional controversies concerning religion leads to the conclusion that they are not so much controversies over the meaning either of the term "religion" or of the concept which it expresses, as they are jurisdictional disputes over the phenomenon or range of phenomena which are considered to constitute legitimately the empirical referent of the term (Spiro, 1969: 87).

In this sense, what constitutes religion in practice or the typical cultural practices designated as manifesting religion is often elusive in terms of arriving at universal and consensual practices of culture which embodies religion in different social contexts. In other words, there is no universal consensus even among scholars of religion concerning the peculiar phenomena to which religion applies.

However, the controversy is perhaps more obtuse with regards to what is or what constitutes religion with reference to the occult, rituals, belief in abstract forces and supernatural forces. In spite of the often clear ambiguity associated with such cultural elements, it is important to equally recognize that much of the controversy in this case may be borne out of the extra-scientific considerations which scientists may consciously or otherwise bring to bear on their studies (see, Spiro, 1969). The major challenge here, however, is mostly brewed by the over-burdening concern to arrive at universal referents or attributes of religion in practical terms which applies through time and space. The quests for such comparative perspectives undermine the peculiarity of religion.

However, a simple way out of the above dilemma is to define religion in terms of the belief in and/or practices associated with supernatural beings. But such a definition is confronted with a Durkheimean rebuttal. The classical French sociologist Emile Durkheim in the bid to arrive at a universal definition and grand narrative of religion argued that the use of the above definition would be tantamount to denying the religious claims of primitive peoples who make no distinction between the natural and supernatural. Closely related to the worry with the definitional universe of the so-called primitive peoples, Durkheim equally questions the definition of religion essentially in terms of the belief in the existence of God since for him Buddhism which is a religion has no such belief (Durkheim, 1954). However, the above earlier observations of Durkheim can easily be dismissed today on a couple of grounds ranging from the pejorative conceptualization of primitive; over-generalization and fascination with establishing universal categories to the wrong perception or reading of Buddhism which has different versions or schools of worship (which Durkheim actually confused with belief system or religious philosophy). In short, Durkheim overlooks the nagging fact that universalism needs not be a necessary condition for the study or comparison of phenomena especially those aligned to or oriented to culture.

Durkheim's headache with the proper definition of religion may have arisen from his own fixation on the integrative role of religion in society. Besides, whatever one may conceive as the role of religion on integration, the *a priori* assumption of integration means in essence a value judgment which undermines the analytical strength of the concept one is studying. While the notion of integration in religion may serve my purpose here in conceptualizing the occult manifested in the *Egbesu* deity among the Ijaw militants as a bastion of solidarity amongst a group dealing with perceived marginalization in the larger Nigerian federation, there is undoubtedly need to understand that the idea of integration in religious practices and beliefs necessarily generates or exists side by side with disintegration. But beyond this simple logic, integration only becomes analytically reliable in terms of epitomizing the attributes peculiar to a given religion and not necessarily as a means of comparison between different religions or even as characteristic of all religions.

The above mentioned worries of Durkheim simply challenge our imaginations in dealing with the arduous job of conceptualizing religion. It also calls attention to the need to avoid strict and perceived universal characteristics to which all religions must conform. Thus, religion is often a study in contradictions since one religious form easily cancels out the cherished canons of belief in another one. Even the popular and common stipulation of such attributes as social solidarity, anxiety reduction, reduction of stress, dealing with or facing unpredictable situations, confidence in the future and after life etc. as the hallmarks of religion do not say much about the peculiar strength or nature of any given religion since other similar cultural practices seen as unreligious may equally perform the above functions or serve the same ends for members of a given society. It is in this sense that I discern wisdom in the admonition of Evans-Pritchard (1954) that rather than get stuck with general questions about what is religion; one should get focused on denoting the main features of a given religion in a given cultural setting. In other words, religion should be studied more from its peculiar socio-cultural context and manifestation than from a broad or generalizing perspective. It is only in this sense that one can give religion an observable and ostensive definition.

Taking the advice of Evans-Pritchard above, Melford Spiro contends,

> Since "religion" is a term with historically rooted meanings, a definition must satisfy not only the criterion of cross-cultural applicability but also the criterion of intra-cultural intuitivity; at the least, it should not be counter-intuitive. For me therefore, any definition of 'religion' which does not include, as a key variable, the belief in superhuman...beings who have power to help or harm man is counter-intuitive (Spiro, 1969: 91).

Along the above lines, it is intellectually stultifying to excise the occult from religion simply because the occult also portends negative or harmful dimensions. Therefore, the occult or magic can stand as manifestations of religion and are not necessarily always negative or evil and unconcerned with other-worldly affairs. In this sense, occult in some cases manifest the classical religious attributes of implying belief in superhuman beings; focus on other-worldliness; and clear spiritual values negotiated mainly through rituals and practices reinforcing and enforcing the connection between the occult and the human beings who subscribe to it.

One critical puzzle in my study of the occult beliefs of the youth militants in the Niger Delta Region of Nigeria is the fact that quite a good number of the these militants are also modern day Christians who ostensibly should have no relationship with the deity which modern Christianity perceives as representing the force of darkness. However, these militants see the conflict as deserving of special sacrifices including subscribing to the deity which they see as not necessarily contradicting of or cancelling out their Christianity. In fact, in a typical case, one of my respondents, a self-confessed former militant stated, "even though I believe in the powers of the *Egbesu* and its importance to our struggle in this country, I am still a Christian. I go to church every Sunday that I am around" [22]. But it must be mentioned here that the belief in the deity within the context of the conflict in the region may be perceived by these Christians as simply a means to an end while their Christianity or beliefs associated with it still remains the ultimate end.

Perhaps a good way of explaining the above is offered by the postulation that, 'although the differentiating characteristic of religion is the belief in superhuman being, it does not follow, moreover that these beings are necessarily objects of ultimate concern. Again, it depends on whether they are viewed as means or ends' (Spiro, 1969: 95). In this case, the *Egbesu* deity may not be of ultimate concern for the militants but the ends to which its existence is sought may be. Given the above mindset, the Christians among the militants may see the deity as a transient object of worship with the power of assisting in the end or desired outcome in the conflict but not really an ultimate or overwhelming concern and thus not reflecting a supernatural end per se.

Essentially the *Egbesu* deity can be located in the ideal normative patterns of the Ijaw who culturally have seen the deity as a critical influence in their lives. In this sense, the relationship between the Ijaw and the deity reflect a crucial characteristic of religion as an institution consisting of culturally patterned interaction with culturally postulated superhuman beings (see Spiro, 1969). Thus, the *Egbesu* represents a process of interaction between the deity and the Ijaw people. Even the invocation of the deity in the conflict by the youth falls within the process of interaction which may bind a people to a given religious practice. In other words, religion is an attribute of social groups and is located within the cultural framework or heritage of social

---

[22] Personal Interview: 14th August 2009, Ekeremo Bayelsa state

groups. It is in the above logic that the Durkheimean contention that there can be no religion without a church (Durkheim, 1954) becomes weak in the face of the realization that religion is a cultural system and can be meaningfully explained within the cultural patterns of a given society.

The invocation of the *Egbesu* deity within the youth's cognitive frame should be seen as aligned to the conceptualization of religion as an invisible order that influences humans and their behaviours or actions. Therefore, the definition of religion as,

> 'a belief in the existence and workings of spiritual beings or divine forces, and the recognition of an invisible order or reality that affects humans and their behavior. This order always has a transcendental, supra-individual dimension and refers to perceived ancestor spirits, creator beings or forces "beyond"'(Abbink, 2014: 85);

seems very germane and largely insightful of the immense influence of religion on life in general in different areas of Africa in spite of the pull of modernity.

Religion as Positive and Collective

Basically what confers the label of socially destructive or constructive provenance on the traditional religious beliefs and practices by Africans is the end to which spiritual power is put. Thus, two individuals with spiritual powers may reflect different outcomes (negative versus positive) for their communities. An individual with an extra-ordinary spiritual power and ability to mediate between the ordinary mortals and the supernatural may in one situation manifest positive or good outcomes on the community (socially constructive) by using his spiritual powers as a rain maker or a healer. In another situation, that same type of individual may opt, due to personal cravings, experiences and even greed to put such powers to negative and evil usage (socially destructive or disruptive) by becoming the repository of evil providing charms, amulets and practices associated with death; physical and economic afflictions and even money making rituals. So what is at stake is not the inherent bad or good nature of the religion or occult but the personal and environmental factors which mediate the exercise of spiritual powers.

In spite of the above, colour often plays a critical role in defining the expected or designed role of religious and occult practices i.e. whether the practice in question is evil or good. However for the occult, the choice is mostly between white and black though red also plays a critical part in some rituals. But there is the binary distinction between white and black used by different social groups in characterizing the nature and intended purpose of the supernatural in the affairs of humans. The usage of the binary distinction between black and white to denote occult or witchcraft practices in Africa and other areas of the world is well documented in ethnography.

But very close to my focus on the Niger Delta region of Nigeria is that even among the Yoruba of Southwestern Nigeria the colour 'black' means essentially evil and is associated with negative occult practices and sorcery. Thus, Joan Wescott in a very illuminating article in the journal '*Africa*' contends that 'black' among the Yoruba is associated with the night and the night in turn is associated with evil,

'it is at night that sorcery and witchcraft are abroad and men are most vulnerable. Some Yoruba say simply that Elegba (the Trickster deity) is painted black because of his wickedness' (Wescott, 1962: 346).

The usage of black to denote evil or negative attribute is more widespread than one would readily imagine and nowhere is the colour bar in this case more pronounced than in the area of beliefs and practices associated with the occult or the supernatural. Another good instance of the above phenomenon is captured in the case of the people of Madagascar where the distinction between white and black is equally couched in terms of the binary opposition between good and evil. According to Leib (1946) the mythical significance of colour among the peoples of Madagascar is that while black is associated with the words: inferior, unpleasant, evil, suspicious, disagreeable, undesirable; white is associated with light, hope, joy, purity. Thus, the colour black denotes things which are evil and undesirable among the peoples of Madagascar.

Perhaps the most illuminating symbolism of colour among social groups is captured in the study of the Ndembu of Angola by Victor Turner. Among the Ndembu, three colours are invested with ritual or symbolic significance in religion. These colours are white, red and black. The outcome of Turner's study of the Ndembu is that the colour white is associated with goodness; purity; lack of misfortune; and more crucially to *'have power'* or *'to be with power'* (Turner, 1969: 58). The colour red in Turner's study of the Ndembus refers especially to 'the blood of witchcraft/sorcery (*mashi awuloji*), for Ndembu witchcraft/sorcery is necrophagous and in anti-witchcraft rites red stands for the blood exposed in such feats' (Turner, 1969: 60). More or less red acts like a medium for conveying power or blood. In another sense, red empowers and activates; hence wooden figurines which have no blood and cannot act can be activated by sorcerers by giving them blood (power) which enables them to move about and kill people (see, Turner, 1969).

But more interesting for me here is the discovery of the ritual significance of the colour black among the Ndembu by Turner (1969). Black or blackness (wuyila) among the Ndembu is associated with badness or evil; lack of luck or impurity; suffering; affliction with diseases and more insightfully, 'witchcraft/sorcery (wuloji), for if your liver is black, you can kill a person, you are bad (muchima neyi wuneyili wukutwesa kujaha

100

muntu, wunatami dehi); on the contrary, if your liver is white, you are good, you laugh with your friends, you are strong together, you prop one another up when you would have failed alone' (Turner, 1969: 60 – 61). In the effort to make meaning of and interpret his findings, Victor Turner posits:

> A brief survey of the senses attributed by informants to 'white' and 'black' respectively indicates that these can mostly be arrayed in a series of antithetical pairs, as for example; goodness/blackness; purity/lacking purity; lacking bad luck/lacking luck; lacking misfortune/misfortune; to be without death/death; life/death; health/disease; laughing with one's friends/witchcraft; to make visible/darkness, etc. (Turner, 1969: 64).

In the above narrative Turner makes the comparison between the meanings symbolically attributed to the colours black and white. In this exercise, the colour white is not just the contrast of black but epitomizes good or positive attributes and desires while the opposite colour black denotes evil or negative attributes and afflictions. However, while the general denotation of good and evil by white and black is given in the foregoing discourse, the acquisition and usage of spiritual powers as obvious from the above is also subject to the binary opposition between black and white. Hence social groups even in the effort to capture the distinction between the various ends to which occult powers serve often use the binary opposition between the white witch and the black witch. In this worldview, occult powers or spiritual powers can either be put to positive (white) use or negative (black) use. The above fine distinction between different uses of spiritual powers is very pertinent in the examination of the occult phenomenon even in the context of conflict and modernity in African societies.

For instance, some communities in the present Edo state of the Niger Delta region of Nigeria often make a distinction between the black and white witches (no reference to racial categories). In the popular imagery in such places, white witches signify good and function as healers, rain makers, peace makers and the community depends on such people or witches for rain during droughts; healing from afflictions including providing antidote to poisons and evil charms. A comparable practice is found in traditional Igbo societies where the *Eze-muo* (head diviner; head-witchdoctor) functions as the repository of guidance and advice (counsel) to the traditional ruler and the community at large in difficult situations and acts as the mouthpiece of the gods and the mediator between the community and its gods and ancestors as well as being the custodian of the village deity. All these functions were considered not just as good or positive but as essential to the continued existence of the community as a social entity. On the other hand, the black witch is seen as embodying evil, enemy of the community and one who uses his spiritual power for negative purposes.

However, the above examples should not be seen as totally confirming the morally ambiguous notion of spiritual power (see, ter Haar and Ellis, 2009). In other words, the automatic assumption that spiritual power is morally ambiguous or ambivalent in Africa is largely wrong since the local/traditional idioms and beliefs in many African societies see white witches as those bound by supernatural and personal forces to do so i.e. use their spiritual power for good. These people are seen as having entered a contract with their personal 'god' or '*chi*' among the Igbo of Nigeria to use their power for good. Failure to do this would in popular imagery result in the death of the white witch concerned or some other severe affliction from the gods. This worldview about the role of the white witch is a commonly shared knowledge in these communities.

Probably confusing the semantic categories and perception of both religion and occult is the juxtaposition of moral leanings and definitions of Christianity especially the Pentecostal brand on the traditional religious worldview of the people. The definition and branding of all aspects of traditional religious practices as negative and evil by latter day Christianity has generated the relative tendency even in popular discourse to consign negative properties to these practices. In this case, the advent of Christianity has fostered an imagination of all aspects of traditional religion as evil and negative among the people of Africa. This process has been finalized by the relatively new Pentecostal churches that have defined these practices as reflecting bad religion or even not religion at all (see, Jenkins and Maier, 1992). The ability to exercise power over these practices or the occult has been purveyed by these churches as critical test of faith.[23] A supposed article of faith that has been swallowed wholesale by contemporary Africans who can hardly make the historical connection between today's social realities and the past of their various societies.

Religion as Neutral and without Prejudice

The argument on the usage of the concept of religion instead of occult and the pejorative inclination in using these concepts in the study of African societies and social realities may actually reflect more of a moralizing intellectualism than a worry with analytical concerns. In fact, Geschiere (1997) has called attention to this highly moralizing view of occult forces. In his words, 'most anthropologists still tend to reduce discourses on witchcraft to an unequivocal opposition between good and evil, even when the local terminology hardly lends itself to this'(Geschiere, 1997: 12). One unintended consequence of adopting a feverish irrationality in viewing the occult in its entirety in Africa is that it continues with the perception of things African or traditional as inherently anti-development,

---

[23] Such exercise is depicted in rituals of destruction of the physical signs of these practices especially burning wood effigies; forests and others said to be representative of the deities behind these practices

backward and unprogressive (see for instance Comaroff and Comaroff, 2003; Bilgin and David, 2002).

Incidentally this frame of reference is often reminiscent of throwing away the baby with the birth water which apart from sponsoring a negative radicalization of society to meet the perceived ideals of modernity deprives us the opportunity to learn lessons from these phenomena. It is rather unfortunate but quite true that, 'to date the cultural heritage of African societies is still unjustly seen by majority of experts merely in terms of development constraints, dominated by characteristics such as rent seeking, informal sector trap, irrational economic actors or the prebend economy, without due regard to its historical roots and its dependency on the global economic system' (Dirk, 2007: 34).

The use of occult here should not be seen as totally in contradiction with religion. I take occult in this case as a particular reflection of religious practice and beliefs. However, while religion when conceived on the moralizing tone as just embodiment of good tends towards collective ownership and beliefs cutting across different social categories in a given community (like *Egbesu* in its ideal state as an Ijaw deity before the Niger Delta conflict); occult privileges religious beliefs and practices as a category that can be approximated and imbued with the desires of a given group or individual (the appropriation and extension of collective beliefs and practices for the benefit of a sub-social group, in this case the youth militants). But more important however, is that I see religion from broader and highly diverse variations. Thus, I subscribe to the anthropological perspective that religion is about the 'existence and causal powers of non-observable entities and agencies. These may be one unique God or many different ones or spirits or ancestors or any combination of these different kinds' (Boyer, 2001: 8). In other words, one sees religion from neither a parochial, universalistic domination or superiority of a given belief system nor moralizing, judgmental and compelling perspectives but rather as more habitualised, varied, contradictory, environmentally nuanced and human agency mediated phenomenon.

The German scholar Kohnert Dirk in reference to the notorious Okija shrine case in Southeastern Nigeria in 2004 has captured succinctly the force behind the denial and assumed bliss of ignorance which many Nigerian elites adopt in viewing the occult. Thus,

> Many Western educated Nigerians considered the continued existence and strength of the country's traditional and informal social control systems as a repulsive contradiction to the country's quest to become a "modern" state with good governance. The words 'shrine' or 'secret cult' assume quasi-automatically a diabolical meaning in the ears of those who advocated good governance and the rule of law. But there is strong evidence that Okija and similar secret cults remain very popular among Nigerians, honoured and feared (Dirk, 2007: 39).

The above sentiments seem reasonable against the realization that the advent of Christianity especially Pentecostalism has engendered the recreation of representation of the notion and perception of the occult by Nigerians in line with the ideal beliefs of the church. Moreover, the educated elites in question are typically those for who education can be defined as a progressive alienation from one's socio-cultural heritage; a fact often associated with the colonial context of Western education in Nigeria (see, Anugwom, 2009). Despite the above, one can still raise concerns about the whole notion of popularity of the 'Okija shrine' or similar cults in contemporary Nigeria which is evidently exaggerated in the views of Dirk. The fact that these cults exist does not automatically confer popularity on them. As a matter of fact, the inroads made by Christianity in the last couple of decades have severely eroded such popularity or wide acceptance. Thus, the occult apart from notoriety in political circles in Nigeria is often a fallback tool in social emergencies nowadays.[24]

In privileging the occult as religion in this study I have simply operationalised the concept within the purview of this particular study. As ter Haar and Ellis (2009) observe what is needed is not to pick a favorite definition of religion from those on offer but rather to formulate a definition that emerges from the context under study. It is actually a requirement of rigour and methodology that definitions are made operational and thus conceptually related and consistent with one's study. Moreover, my definition seeks to privilege the examination of the practices associated with *Egbesu* among the militants in the Niger Delta without the burden of bias or an a priori belief or expectation that they are negative. The use of a concept that is defined as neutral and not from a moral pedestal is perhaps in order since the *Egbesu* may as well be considered to have both positive and negative dimensions depending essentially on which side of the divide one belongs.

In other words, the youth militants perceive the *Egbesu* as a potent social constructive force deployed in the war against the marginalization visited on the oil producing communities by the Nigerian government and TNOCs. In this sense, it becomes a god of justice and on the side of the socially marginalized. However, the other parties in the conflict, the government forces and the TNOCs may have the feeling that *Egbesu* is socially destructive or disruptive since it generates the psychological fervor and courage driving the youth militants. Incidentally the older members of the communities as we shall see view the usage of the deity in new ways by the youth as not

---

[24] Even in the area of both traditional and modern healing, people often fall back on the traditional or occult when the ailment has defied western remedies. This is exactly why ailments that have no known or easy cure like HIV/AIDS; asthma; stroke; diabetes etc. have created a boom for alternative or traditional healing or witchcraft in modern Africa. The work of Adam Ashforth (2005) in Soweto, South Africa; Kaori Sugishita (2009) on ng'anga in Lusaka, Zambia among others make interesting reading here

totally conforming to the ideal perception of the role and essence of the deity. This suggests the appropriation of the deity by the youth militants (a refashioning of the deity to suit present pressing needs).

In line with the foregoing narratives the usage of the occult here does not so much embody the signaling of socially destructive or disruptive beliefs or practice as it signifies fundamental appropriation of a religious belief system and its extension to cover the new needs and intentions defined solely by the youth militants in the Niger Delta. Incidentally the occult belief system which is most despised in some quarters (see, Tebbe, 2007 for a typical illustration) may unwittingly provide the needed remedies to the negative and destructive violence associated with the occult in modern Africa. It is only reasonable that a conceptualization of the occult as neutral and equally embodied with positive attributes implicates it as a reliable vehicle towards ensuring peace and solidarity as well as eliminating violence in African societies.

As the history of traditional Africa shows, the occult which also represents a belief and thought process was vital in the ability of Africans to come to terms with and tame negative and destructive elements in their environment. This potential is equally possible in the modern African society and demands a more constructive engagement or understanding of the phenomenon. As Dirk (2007: 37) aptly contends,

African religious systems provided a framework for valuable indigenous solutions to current problems of contemporary life, for example within the realm of increasing violence of non-state actors, including the problem of witchcraft violence. Besides, under certain conditions, they might provide the outside world with an inspiring new dimension of philosophic thought and emancipative action, for example, within the realm of conflict resolution and reconciliation (Dirk, 2007: 37).

The Occult in Religion

Perhaps the clearest link of the occult practices by youth militants in Nigeria to the religious may be seen not in the often wrongly conceptualized notion of rationality as simply modernization but rather in the emotive and visionary attributes of religion. In this case, religion embodies human emotions and encapsulates the vision of the believers about what the world should or ought to be. Therefore, the occult may signify both rejection of the existing *status quo* and more crucially an indicator of the fantasies or visions of what ought to be. The revision of the *Egbesu* deity by youth militants, some of who are Christians point to a frustration with and rejection of the political economy of oil exploitation in Nigeria but more critically represents an urge for a desired state of affairs where the society is predicated and structured on a pan-Ijaw social idiom.

Be that as it may, the reluctance to treat the occult as part and parcel of African religion would really indicate either a tendency towards denial or the western influenced fantasization of the African past. Therefore, the occult is not just an embodiment of religion in Africa and elsewhere for that matter but rather a pervasive religious practice in the African context. Thus, 'occult belief systems in Africa reflect a cultural process which is not at all limited to remote places in the hinterland, but is based on African traditional religions and shaped by current linkages between transnational social spaces in a globalised world' (Dirk, 2007: 37).

Despite the above, one may be tempted to see the invocation of the *Egbesu* deity by Ijaw youth militants in the Niger Delta as resembling the antithesis of modernity. In this case even the enlightened youth among the militants, in spite of Christianity, subscribe to efficacy or enduring strength of the deity and see it as a medium for addressing the marginalization of the people of the region. Thus, the militants see the appropriation of the

Egbesu as instrumental in negotiating and coming to terms with modernity as represented by the government and the TNOCs.

The appropriation of the *Egbesu* apart from embodying the aspirations of the youth for a better future may equally underline a gnawing need to deal with the fears and unpredictability of the present. There is nothing original or new about the foregoing idea. In his famous study of the Trobriand Islands, Malinouski for instance saw the appeal to the supernatural as an exit negotiation from unpredictability by the Islanders. Even though the Trobriand Islands analogy may resemble a throw-back to the past, there is evidence to believe that beliefs in supernatural power has gone full circle and there is a certain air of resurgence of spirituality and religion in different guises today. But more contemporary is the revealing study of Peter Geschiere in postcolonial Cameroonian society. It is interesting that he notes,

> To many Westerners, it seems self-evident that the belief in witchcraft or sorcery is something "traditional" that will automatically disappear with modernization. But this stereotype does not fit with actual developments in Africa today. Throughout the continent, discourses on sorcery or witchcraft are intertwined, often in quite surprising ways, with modern changes (Geschiere, 1997: 2).

In the above sense, occult, sorcery or witchcraft have refused to become practically anachronistic but rather exists in the shadows of even the most westernized African society. The penchant of Pentecostal preachers in the continent to build their reputation and perceived supernatural powers around the ability to overpower the occult or liberate people from sorcery and witch craft (see, Anugwom, 2010) typically shows the continuing influence such phenomenon exerts in modern Africa. This fact which has won converts and support for Pentecostal ministries illustrate clearly the futility of drawing diametric opposition or separation between the modern and the occult in lived-reality of people.

However, in approaching the occult narrative in Africa one should be wary of the fact that it is an area which abounds with fertile imaginations (rumours and bogus tales); a sphere for discrediting of political and business enemies or rivals (invocation of occult source of riches even where hardly possible can tarnish one's social image and serve one's rival's need to leverage opportunity or narrow the distance in achievement); and equally operates in the psychological realm (invocation to create courage based on belief of occult mediated invincibility; to create fear and exert negative influence on the other party). Apart from the above, one should recognize that occult and witchcraft narratives as Geschiere (1997) argues are the subject of constant reformulations and recreations often generated by need to signify politico-economic changes or to even gain control over them.

Geschiere (1997) has shown that the obsession with witchcraft haunts the elites in Africa as much as the rest of the population. Therefore, the phenomenon of sorcery or occult is not just a marker for the less privileged or uneducated or even those totally at the margin of the socio-economic process in the society. However, the goals and purposes of invocation and practice of occult may differ between different social classes in the society and between the elites and the rest of the population.

A good number of students of African philosophy and religion have no qualms whatsoever about seeing what is called the occult or occult practices and beliefs as part of the religious universe of societies in Africa. The Dutch philosopher cum religious scholar Wim van Binsbergen in his study of Northeastern Botswana broadly divided its religious universe into the churches of the spirit and mediumistic sangoma cult lodges which he saw as two dominant religious expressions there (van Binsbergen, 1991). But beyond mere distinction van Binsbergen sees the sangoma which is a form of ancestor worship or more appropriately ancestor veneration and the Christian idiom of the churches as functioning to facilitate the adaptation of the worshippers or believers to the social and economic challenges of living. Without doubt, the ancestors were considered significant and key intermediaries to the Supreme Being by a lot of African societies. Therefore, while there are differences in the ancestor cult or figure in each community, a general notion of a Supreme Being known by different names and whose link with the ordinary mortals were through the deities and ancestors existed.

In such a situation, deities acquired immediacy and accessibility that often leads the uninitiated to think about an African society without the notion of the Supreme Being. But much closer to the fundamental thinking of Christianity on the accessibility and mediation of heavenly angels and forces for all true believers irrespective of race or language, the deities were equally seen as collectively owned and reflective of the religious conscience of the social group concerned. However, ancestors as important as they are seem more limited to sub-social groups and often approached in general terms. Thus, it is common to make reference to 'our ancestors' rather than to a specific ancestor except in situations where the idiom of origin of a given group implicates a known ancestor or the ancestor has been extra-ordinarily distinguished in the social myth of the group. The ancestors are essentially mediators of the spiritual and existential needs of the living and thus vital in the bid to negotiate favours from deities and the Supreme Being (usually approached through the deities).

While one appreciates the pessimism regarding the efficacy of the occult in real life situations in Africa, there are countless narratives which tend to portray occult or sorcery influences and power in Africa. Apart from the frenzied reports one gets now and then of supernatural power gone amok in modern Africa[25], there are other indications of the belief in the efficacy of these even by non-Africans[26]. However, the South African Pagan Rights Alliance (SAPRA) in one of its press releases in 2009 did a good summary of the imaginations of the real manifestations of negative occult menace in different parts of Africa (SAPRA, 2009). Thus: a granny is killed in her home in Mulemwana near Qumbu, Eastern Cape South Africa on suspicion of witchcraft; a gang dismembers an albino boy in Buyumbura Burundi on a crime linked to witchcraft; in Kenya, elders from Kilifi seek protection from youth who kill old people on the suspicion they are witches; in the Nigerian state of Akwa Ibom, children are victims of a deadly witchcraft purge; witches put to death in Papua New Guinea (they were burnt, stoned, slashed, poisoned or hanged and range from the young to the old and more often than not they were women); an uncle abandons niece and nephew for refusing to take heed of his advice to stop practicing witchcraft in Salima, Malawi etc. But apart from the above which may inform the thinking that occult and witchcraft embody essentially negative powers and also supports the notion that tensions and pressures of modernity make occult imaginations alluring across Africa, there is also the sobering report of the positive and efficacious deployment of occult in the continent. For instance, in the growing areas of traditional healing practices the use of roots and herbs guided by what may be seen as occult like healing cults have mediated healthcare especially in remote and rural areas (see Sugishita, 2009 for a good discussion of this in the case of Zambia).

---

[25] There is always a rich dosage of this in the press releases of the South Africa Pagan Rights Alliance – SAPRA on
http://www.paganrightsalliance.org/press.html
[26] Actually the fact is that occult imaginations are widespread global phenomena which takes different forms in different societies. Even in the most advanced societies such religious sects like the Davidians in the U.S for instance approximate every definition of the negative side of occult practices. So occult is not peculiarly African or developing world phenomenon

Once more, van Binsbergen provides insight from his own personal experience while on fieldwork in Botswana. Thus, 'against the sorcery attacks we were so obviously victim to, he supplied magical substances with which to doctor our yard and bodies; the daily rites through which to administer them, helped us through our most distressful weeks in Francistown' (van Binsbergen, 1991: 315). He was making reference in the quotation to a Zulu who after a 26 year career as a deep water cabin steward came back home to become a traditional healer on the call of his ancestors. Without doubt there are numerous cases of Smart Gumede (the Zulu in van Binsbergen's story) in so many places in modern Africa. These people use occult powers, magic or white witchcraft to impact positively on the daily lives of people and of course to an extent facilitate the negotiation of the often daunting challenges and pressures of modernity in the continent.

The rise of negative occult imaginations and sorcery should be related primarily to the upsurge in Pentecostal and spirit churches which apart from exploiting their perceived spiritual powers over occult are responsible in the first place for implanting (in some cases)and sustaining the notions of the occult in people's consciousness and heightening (in other cases) the notions of the occult as totally destructive, evil, negative and repellant in the consciousness of their members and even beyond. Even though a proper census has not been carried out, the reported incidences of negative occult practices and imaginations would no doubt be associated with urban areas and rural enclaves under the siege of new Christianity. The power over the occult and witchcraft and a claim of the ability to deal with all manner of afflictions remain critical marketing points of the Pentecostal churches in Africa (see, Anugwom, 2010; Gifford, 1987).

Equally a factor in the upsurge is the whole gamut of new challenges[27] thrown up by modernity and the increasing voiding of socio-economic linkages, networks and traditional support systems by modernity induced development as well as the fierce zero-sum game in political and economic spheres in modern Africa. In the above regard, the views of the Comaroffs (1999) provide a crucial perspective on the upsurge of occult imaginations in Africa. But while occult imageries and idioms become even more relevant in the political sphere (see, Geschiere, 1997) there is need to consider that occult especially the negative evil powers it promises remain very attractive to those who are marginal to or consistently jam brick walls in the attempt to negotiate economic or political success. A typical case in point here is the upsurge in allegations of people relying on money making rituals in their businesses or even politicians demonizing opponents as witches or occult practitioners or even the reported case of a governor in Southwestern Nigeria who enforced occult oath taking on commissioners and house of assembly members in order to be assured of their loyalty and ensure that they would not impeach him (see, Alausa, 2009). In spite of the fact that these stories sound exotic and thus attractive one needs to be cautioned that occult and witchcraft allegations, even where totally baseless have been invented to gain advantages over competition and opponents or even to mud sling someone or rubbish his achievements (see, also Geschiere, 1997 on the manipulative usage of occult imaginations).

Incidentally the obvious vibrancy of occult in African societies gnaws at a most fundamental assumption of the modernization ideology regarding development in the continent. It counteracts the sentiments that, 'modernization would inevitably rationalize both social processes and human beliefs.

---

[27] For instance voiding traditional economic niches; dispossession through environmental degradation of the rights of farmers to meaningful living by depending on their lands and resources therein

This also holds for "traditional" African religions, and particularly for the occult belief, i.e. the belief in magic and witchcraft, characterized by modernists as superstition' (Dirk, 2007: 34). In spite of the valuable insight provided by the above statement, it still raises another problem with the modernists' view of the occult in Africa which is that of the assumption of irrationality. Therefore, it is important to point out that the irrationality of religion can only be meaningful when conceptualized as a universal characteristic of religions since no religion anywhere in the world is based on the type of wholesome objectivity and dispassion one finds in science.

Without doubt, some religions may claim more rationality on this score than others but all of them are marked by different degrees of what may be considered irrationality in the frame of the type of rationality invoked by modern science. Therefore, African traditional religion whether denoted as ancestor veneration or occult is as irrational as the other forms of religion in the world. However, the concept of rationality in spite of its overwhelming modern taint should be gauged on the basis of what makes sense and realistically mediate experience in any given socio-cultural context. In this sense, some traditional African religious practices or occult practices may in fact be imbued with more rationality and objective goals and knowledge than some elements of western modernity[28].

---

[28] A good case here is the art of rainmaking in traditional African society. Also, the works of Geschiere (1997) and Crick (1979) aptly demonstrate that some of the actions of individuals even in western societies seen as quite normal can be perceived as equally imbued with "irrationality" and "witchcraft" as some people are wont to label the occult in Africa. Therefore, while Geschiere draws an interesting similarity between the African marabouts and the role attributed to public relations experts in American politics; Crick sees the characteristic traits supposedly personifying the African witches as equally manifest in some major degrees in the case of the forgetful, absent-minded and ill-clad professor in western societies. Therefore, the argument that the difference between the rationality of African witchcraft beliefs and western forms of reasoning lies more in the degree of

its reduction than necessarily in the degree of rationality per se (see, Dirk, 2007) seems pertinent.

Chapter Six

Occult Manifestations in the Niger Delta

The *Egbesu* is the god of warfare and this god is of Ijaw origin in the Niger Delta region of Nigeria. From time immemorial the deity has been used by the Ijaws as a spiritual foundation for combating evil. Our forefathers always say that the *Egbesu* is as old as mankind itself. Given this, a date of existence cannot be associated with the *Egbesu* deity. After all, the church goers say that their God has no beginning and no end, I believe so with the *Egbesu* deity[29].

Re-imagining the Occult: Nature of the *Egbesu* as Deity and Destiny in the Niger Delta

Though this study assumes a generalized notion of the occult typified by the *Egbesu* deity of the Ijaw now common among many of the militant organizations in the Niger Delta, it must be mentioned that the influence of the occult emerged quite early in the Niger Delta conflict. In fact, one of the most daring militant groups in the 1990s which can be seen as the forerunner of the present Movement for the Emancipation of the Niger Delta (MEND)[30] is the *Egbesu* Boys of Africa (EBA) which reportedly was invested with the power of invincibility by the *Egbesu* deity. In fact, the resilience of the group in skirmishes

---

[29] Personal Interview with Preye Dappa, 23 year old boat mechanic in Buguma, Rivers state; 12th August 2009

[30] Based on recent utterances credited to the MEND this year (2016), the group, it would appear has embraced dialogue as a solution to the Niger Delta problem. It has been very vocal in condemning the use of violence recently by other nascent militant groups. One of these new groups which is equally potent and violent is the Niger Delta Avengers (NDA) which has launched a spate of bombing campaigns on oil installations in the region since the beginning of 2016.

with the security agencies in the swamps and creeks of the Niger Delta soon created the myth in popular culture that the members of the group can submerge under water for a whole day or swim below the water surface for over ten kilometers without coming up for air. These feats were seen as explaining the relative failure of the security forces to check mate the group. The connection between the *Egbesu* Boys and the *Egbesu* deity is perhaps given more impetus by the fact that the group emerged as a spiritual wing of the Ijaw youth. According to Best and von Kemedi (2005: 18), 'the Egbesu Boys initially emerged as an Ijaw religious cultural group, but subsequently took up arms in order to challenge perceived injustice caused by the exploitation of oil resources in Ijaw land and the Niger Delta by the Nigerian state and multi-national corporations'.

As if to reinforce the foregoing contention about the emergence of the *Egbesu* Deity within the context of the oil conflict in the Niger Delta, a few of the respondents I spoke to pinpointed the year 1999 and the Odi massacre[31] in Bayelsa state as marking the entry of the *Egbesu* into the fray. Thus: "In my time, I never knew the deity existed but during General Obasanjo's regime an event took place in Odi in Bayelsa. An Ijaw man by name Ogoriba was arrested by the military but an Ijaw chief suggested that the deity be used to go and rescue the man that is in captivity"[32]. In a further confirmatory note,

---

[31] Odi was the site of one of the most dastardly acts of suppression against the Niger Delta population. It was the site of the killing of hundreds of civilians including women and children by Nigerian soldiers acting on orders from above on the 20th of November 1999. Even though the government put the figures of those killed at a modest 43 civilians and 8 soldiers; the Human Rights Watch (1999) thinks otherwise and contends that the soldiers must have killed tens of unarmed civilians and that figures of several hundred dead is plausible. The massacre had resulted from the killing of seven policemen sent on duty to the community by suspected militants operating there. At the end of the shooting and burning carried out by the army only about two buildings were left standing.

[32] Personal Interview with a 31 year old high school dropout in Kaiama on 12th August 2009

another respondent, Ibiam Faka an ex-militant fighter stated, "not much have been happening because all we heard were stories about the powers of the *Egbesu* deity. The deity has not really been in use until 1999 when Odi was attacked by the federal government. That was when we experienced the powers of the deity"[33].

In spite of the above sentiments, I must point out that my efforts to capture the *Egbesu* deity and the rituals webbed around it in diachronic terms were not as successful as I would have imagined. Part of the frustration implied in this stemmed from the secrecy surrounding the deity and more critically the concern of my informants especially youth militants about security. However, I pieced out some information from my interactions with the militants, the old men who are custodians of culture and gate-keepers and the scanty literature available. As already pointed out, the Egbesu deity's presence in the conflict was first heralded by the arrival of the Egbesu Boys of Africa (EBA) in the forefront of the conflict in the delta in the 1990s. EBA is often identified as the military wing of the Ijaw Youth Council and was first led by the popular warlord Mujaheed Asari-Dokubo, a law college drop-out and converted Muslim (see, Danish Immigration Service, 2005). It must be pointed out however that another and perhaps more reliable account in a Nigerian Newspaper by Ollor-Obari (1998, cf. Obi, 2001) sees the EBA as led by one Alex Preye. The leadership of the organization by Dokubo may have been shortly before or immediately after Preye given the rapid dynamism and mutation of the militant groups in the region especially at the height of the conflict between the late 1990s and 2008. Asari Dokubo nonetheless led the IYC for some period of time. Actually, one of the state governors in the region in the bid to gain more control over the increasingly popular IYC backed Asari Dokubo to become the President between 2001 and 2003 when he

---

[33] Personal Interview, 14th August 2009, Ekeremor, Bayelsa State

119

stepped down as a result of pressures from other senior members of the group (see, Best and von Kemedi, 2005).

Despite the foregoing account, the establishment of any reliable and formal line of association between the EBA and the IYC has been difficult. The EBA fizzled out between 2003 and 2004 and literally left the stage for Asari Dokubo's Niger Delta Peoples Volunteer Force (NDPVF) and the Niger Delta Vigilantes (NDV) of Ateke Tom. However, it should be noted once more that the militant groups given the nature of their activities and the exigency to protect their members as well as the often abrupt dynamism of youth agency are usually very mutative and continuously recombining in the pursuit of their goals. Thus, while Asari's group became formally dissolved following the peace agreement with the Obasanjo government in the mid-2000s, some elements of this group are now functioning in the MEND which itself is another study in militant confederacy.

Be that as it may, there is unconfirmed speculation that the leader of the Egbesu Boys died in 2001 and was never replaced. While the authenticity of this account cannot be confirmed, the early 2000s, as already pointed out, was consistent with the decline of the EBA from the forefront of the Niger Delta struggle. In spite of the above, there is what is known as the Supreme Egbesu Assembly (SEA) which is the umbrella organization of various Ijaw groups and organizations subscribing to the *Egbesu* belief. The SEA is seen as the spiritual arm of the IYC and is assumed to be led by the IYC leader at the same time. Ideally, as the CDMS (2003) reports the High Priest is consulted before any major operation and the executive members of the EBA include underlings of the Priest. These underlings are expected to provide spiritual cover as the operation is on-going. This practice falls in line with the notion that occult powers need to be regularly appeased or re-energised in order to maintain potency.

The *Egbesu* (also pronounced and spelt as *Egbisu*) made a re-entry into the Niger delta conflict scene with the EBA who openly claimed the power of invincibility as a result of the blessing of the *Egbesu*. It was common for these militants to boast that because of the powers of *Egbesu* the bullets of government forces have no power over them. The EBA continued to hug the headlines of the reports of the conflict in the Niger Delta up until the mid-2004 when the emerging coalition of forces under the MEND began to crystallize. The EBA was active in the six states of the Niger Delta with Ijaw communities viz. Rivers, Bayelsa, (the most dominant in this regard and mostly Ijaw population; in fact the Ijaw almost make up the entire Bayelsa state), Akwa Ibom, Edo, Ondo, and Delta. However, the Bayelsa state town of Amabolou in the Ekeremor LGA is seen as the traditional headquarters of the deity and the EBA (see, CDMS, 2003; Aimaize and Oyadongha, 2005; IRB of Canada, 2006). Predictably, the Ekeremor base is also viewed as the location of the traditional *Egbesu* shrine presided over by a High Priest. The consensus of opinion among the FGD respondents is that Amabolou (Amabulu) in Ekeremor LGA of Bayelsa State is the hometown of the overall priest of the Egbesu in the person of His Royal Majesty Augustine Ebikeme Perekere the 6th of Oporomo Kingdom[34].

As is the practice with this type of belief system, the High priest is the mediator between the people and the deity or god. Therefore, the High Priest communes with and speaks on behalf of the deity and he is also in charge of delivering the services of initiating people and providing spiritual guidance to the initiated. However, respondents also indicated that the *Egbesu* is dispersed among various other communities and have other priests who are supposedly subservient to the overall chief priest. Some of these other locations mentioned by the respondents include:

---

[34] FGDs in Nembe, and Ekeremor in Bayelsa state and Buguma in River State on 29, 30 and 31 of May 2008.

121

a. Kaiama in Kolokuma/Opokuma LGA in Bayelsa state (actually one of the respondents in Gbaram, a retired school teacher and community leader was of the opinion that this was used by the famous Isaac Jasper Adaka Boro)

b. Egbema[35] in Delta state (which some of the respondents said was the Delta state headquarters of the deity).

c. Gbaran (Gbarain) in Southern Ijaw LGA of Bayelsa State

d. Amabolou (Amabulu) in Ekeremor LGA of Bayelsa State which is the hometown of the overall Chief Priest of the Egbesu

e. Nembe

f. Okrika Mainland

g. Polokuma and Opokuma

h. Agalabiri

i. Buguma

j. Arugbo Kingdom in Ondo State

Incidentally, majority of our respondents from Ekeremor boldly claimed superior allegiance to the deity often bordering on pride. Hence, "Ekeremor, my community is the most prominent and every Ijaw community is afraid of us. Other communities are Odi and Sagbama. In fact, all Ijaw communities are in one way or the other strong believers in the *Egbesu* deity"[36]. However, on a slightly different note, a 72 year old community leader from Nembe contended, "any Ijaw community that does

---

[35] Egbema lies in the West of the influential Benin river in the North of the present Delta State and is administratively located in the Warri North LGA. Although often seen as located in the geographical fringe of the Niger Delta, Egbema has a strong and vibrant Ijaw cultural identity and is seen as comprising migrants from other Ijaw groups like the Mein, Iduwini and even Ekeremor (see, Alagoa, 2005). Incidentally Egbema was the known operational base of the Niger Delta Freedom Fighters (NDFF) one of the dreaded youth militant groups which also engaged in kidnapping of oil workers prior to the 2009/2010 amnesty programme.

[36] Personal Interview with a militant in Ekeremor, Bayelsa state, 14th August 2009

not have the presence of the *Egbesu* deity in it must be a very weak community. I know that my community by name Nembe is prominent with this belief as well as Ekeremor and Odi"[37]. The above does not necessarily undermine the claims of Ekeremor (which had almost total consensus among the FGD participants in the three locations) as much as it underlines the fact that the *Egbesu* deity may be a much more common phenomenon among the Ijaw than one would think.

The secrecy surrounding the *Egbesu* deity and the often ambiguous role it plays stem really from the fact that occult matters are hardly discussed openly. In the traditional Ijaw and even in most other African societies such things are usually shrouded in secrecy and mystery. Incidentally such practices relate the esoteric to the spiritual. In other words, the more mysterious and secretive things appear, the more potent they are perceived in local imagery. After all, the notion of secret society under which rubric such things exist essentially entails that they are not open to all comers. However, secrecy should not be equated with evil or repugnant and inhuman practices but rather indicates that in such things a rite of passage (initiation) is required in order to access the inner workings of the practice in question. Typically, the initiated maintain the secrets of the organization as it confers on them some social power. As a result, some of the people who would wish to talk about the deity are those far from it and those inside or near it would earnestly try to preserve the secrecy on which the mystery of the deity depends and which equally confers some social powers on them as the elect.

All the same some of our respondents threw light on issues of worship, initiation and practices associated with the *Egbesu* Deity. These sentiments include:

---

[37] Personal Interview with Chief O.O Benson in Nembe, Bayelsa state, 15th August 2009

In Ijaw land, an unclean person cannot worship *Egbesu* or come to *Egbesu* deity for any form of assistance without first, confessing his sins. After a sincere confession and a commitment to uphold righteousness and truth in times of strife and conflict, you will be protected within the circumstances you find yourself. The chief priest of *Egbesu* is known by so many names like *Egbesu, Dirimo-Asain, Ako-Oru, and Agadagba – Oru*[38].

But as if to confirm the fact that only core devotees of the deity can be much detailed about the worship of the deity, another respondent argued, "the only way you can worship *Egbesu* is to become a devoted member of the *Egbesu* cult and that means an oath to defend your fatherland even with your life. The issue of worship might come in during the process of initiation into the *Egbesu* cult, which entails a lot of rituals that is the exclusive reserve of the *Egbesu* cult members only. After these rituals, the member is expected to obey some natural laws so as to be in harmony with the gods"[39]. Other interesting sentiments from the respondents along this line include, "I will not call it worship. At least we are told that all the rules and procedures are still kept just like our forefathers did. There is always an initiation into the cult and the much I can say is that at the peak of this initiation you will be soaked in water that has been prepared already for the purpose of the initiation. After the bath with the water, you are more or less ready for battle"[40]. But Chief Benson, a 72 year old community leader in Nembe in a more poignant note contends:

> You worship it when you are initiated into the group. For the deity to dwell in you, there are rules and regulations you must

---

[38] Personal Interview with Abi, a secondary school dropout and boat operator in Buguma, 13th August 2009

[39] Personal Interview with Preye Dappa, boat engine mechanic in Buguma, 12th August 2009

[40] Personal Interview with Godbless Miebi, a high school dropout and security guard in an oil firm in Kaiama

meet. We were told that our forefathers did not as much as use one bucket with women. That is how difficult living with the deity can be. The initiation process is also an interesting one. But only those who dare to taste it can tell the story and only they are allowed to know[41].

In spite of the above somewhat ambivalence of opinion, one gathered some interesting details about the worship and observances of the Deity from the FGDs in these communities. These opinions can be summarized thus:

i. **Colour**: Incidentally the *Egbesu* obeys the well-known binary classification between evil and good represented also in the colours black and white. Thus, as the participants in the FGDs agreed the *Egbesu* colour is white which symbolizes peace, equality, fairness and justice.

ii. **Dress Code**: The dress code of the deity is also built around white. So in approaching or appearing before the deity the dress code is:

a. White singlet or vest

b. White handkerchief

c. White shorts

d. *Abuluku* (short white native dress used in covering the waist)

e. White flags

f. White headband and hand band

iii. **Observances:** Just like any other deity with worshippers, the *Egbesu* demand certain observances from the warriors in order to ensure that they have the powers of the deity and can come back alive and victorious. These observances which are equally captured in the individual opinions of those interviewed in other locations in Ijaw land include:

a. Consultation of the oracle or deity before commencement of hostilities

---

[41] Personal Interview, 15th August, 2009

    b. Abstinence from cooked food, women and all things considered unsacred like intimate engagement with a woman who is menstruating. Some respondents mentioned the eating of things like snail and pork as also not acceptable

    c. Chanting of war songs and praises of *Egbesu* just before engaging the enemy. This is really nothing strange since the use of war songs have a universal appeal. Even the early armies of Western societies often marched to the tune of music as they went to engage the enemies. This fact was perhaps captured lightly in the popular Indiana Jones film where the commander of a German army was very much enamored with the music of Wagner that he could not embark on any war march without the regimental musician playing the music of Wagner.

    d. Sanctification of the warriors before they go out for war. This is usually done by the *Egbesu* priests. Apart from the use of water, invocation and other ritual expressions, a key element of the process was the purification of amulets or talisman which the warriors wear and which keep the *Egbesu* power with them always. Those who have come close to the militants would have observed the widespread use of these things.

    e. The consultation of the oracle provides guidance for onward movement and action. Actually this was also widespread in the sense that the blessing or approval of the deity was often sought before the group embarks on any encounter with the enemies of the Ijaw. In some militant camps, there were resident *Egbesu* priests and shrines from which militants derive power regularly and which also protected the camp and its members from prying eyes and from the soldiers of the federal government.

    f. Warriors who desire the unflinching support of the deity must obey all its rules and regulations including not engaging in piracy, not stealing and generally not abusing the privilege of power[42]

In spite of what may still seem like a paucity of information, what is obvious is that the *Egbesu* was and is (still) a traditional deity embraced by Ijaw people and which predates the colonial intervention by the British. It was generally subscribed to by the Ijaw, hence all Ijaw citizens of both sexes are ordinarily seen as belonging to and venerating the deity. The concept of the "Egbesu" according to the Danish Immigration Services (2005) joint report of a fact finding mission stems from a system of beliefs and from the god of war among the Ijaw in Southern Nigeria. Therefore, the *Egbesu* is a common property of the over five hundred Ijaw communities in the Niger Delta region. In the prevailing imageries of the youth militants the *Egbesu* is simply the god of war and also the embodiment of truth and justice in the land of the Ijaw. In their mindset *Egbesu* supports their acts of violence because it is angry over the pollution of Ijaw land and the exploitation and marginalization of the Ijaw in the Nigerian state.

Historically, the *Egbesu* is the deity of the Ijaw people seen as symbolizing the triumph of good over evil or freedom and liberation over captivity. This imagery of the *Egbesu* is somehow quite widespread among many Ijaw communities. Thus, "the *Egbesu* deity has and will always mean the same thing to the Ijaw man both the living and the dead. It means the upholder of justice and the protector of the Ijaw kingdom"[43]. However the deity is also often captured as a god of warfare though by extension. The *Egbesu's* divine force is symbolized by the leopard, an animal dreaded all over Africa for its strength and stalking ability. Incidentally the *Egbesu* deity and its cults suffered predictable decline after the British overcame the Ijaw and

---

[42] Derived from the FGDs in Nembe, Ekeremor and Buguma held on 29th, 30th and 31st of August 2009.

[43] Personal Interview, Michael Dombei, a 67 year old contractor in Buguma, 12th August 2009.

occupied their land as part of the colonizing mission of the British in Nigeria (see, Francis, 2005). This fact was as much acknowledged by a good number of the respondents. Typical of this is the view that:

> The *Egbesu* deity has protected Ijaw kingdom and communities for a very long time. History has it that the last time the deity was in active mood before this present time was during the occupation and subsequent colonialization of not only the Ijaw kingdom but the entire Nigeria by the British. During this time, the *Egbesu* deity was called upon to defend the land, but not much of its rules were kept so the power declined and the British successfully occupied the lands. Ever since no one can recall the deity being called into action until 1999[44].

What emanates from this is that the *Egbesu* is captured in the people's imagination as a protective phenomenon i.e. a supernatural force that shields the Ijaw from evil and mediates between them and outside enemies. In this sense, Moses Siloko Siasia, a 53 year old businessman opined,

> According to my forefathers, *Egbesu* is the god of warfare of the Ijaw people and the people believe in its powers to protect them. The origin of the *Egbesu* deity cannot be traced to any epoch or time in history but is believed to have been passed on from one generation to another. *Egbesu* is a retributive god that fights evil in the land. In recent times, young men now use *Egbesu* deity as a protection to fight against the exploitation of Niger Delta area by the Nigeria government and the emancipation of Ijaw people[45].

---

[44] Personal Interview with Preye Dappa-Silva in Buguma, 12th August 2009

[45] Personal Interview on 11th August 2009 in Grand Brass, Bayelsa state

However, some writers like Cyril Obi who has written extensively on the Niger Delta sees the embrace of the *Egbesu* by youth militants as consistent with the urge to seek legitimacy by embracing local and popular idioms (Obi, 2001). He goes on to see the *Egbesu* deity and the *Ogele* (traditional celebration of life and solidarity in Ijaw using dance and songs) as two examples of the above. While there is evident substance in the above view, it all the same narrows down the influence of the *Egbesu* within the Ijaw socio-cultural worldview especially in the context of conflict or perceived injustice. This view is often contradicted by the sentiments of the respondents. For instance, "for the Ijaw people the diety will continue to be the Supreme Being and the upholder of truth and justice in Ijaw land. Therefore, the *Egbesu* deity has never changed from its meaning right from time immemorial"[46]. Perhaps the above sentiments are re-echoed in the submission of another respondent, "our forefathers handed it down to us and it meant a lot to them. It was the *Egbesu* deity that had kept the Ijaw land from being taken over by enemies and it is still doing the same duty today"[47].

Probably catapulting the importance of the *Egbesu* is that it is seen as the source of the strength and invincibility of the youth militants. In general, the young recruits are initiated into the *Egbesu* (a sort of re-awakening of the rite of passage since all free born Ijaws are automatically subjects of the deity and empowered with the spiritual power of the deity) which involves the use of scarification on the body by priests of the deity in the various cults and shrines of the deity. Apart from the use of scarification, physical presence of the deity is equally portrayed through the wearing of amulets; painting of the faces (though the militants prefer fighting with faces covered); and use of charms of various types which are aimed at making one bullet-

---

[46] Personal Interview with Preye Dappa-Silva in Buguma, 12th August 2009

[47] Personal Interview with Chief Akuro Diete-Spiff, a 69 year old self-employed community leader in Grand Brass, 11th August 2009.

proof or invincible. Perhaps, the above over-arching role of the *Egbesu* may provide justification for the use of violence but like the leopard, the deity is deemed to manifest formidable adversary in the militants.

Therefore, it would appear that in spite of the assumed general ownership of the *Egbesu* by all Ijaws, the conflict has generated the need for a process of initiation (may be a form of re-energizing the potency of the deity) for the youth militants. This should not be surprising entirely since the process of a rite based re-energisation or re-activization of a deity's power is common really among different groups in the South of Nigeria. In fact, this process is seen as moving the supernatural from a redundant or idle mode to active mode which a conflict demands. Thus, the militants undergo the initiations (or process of re-activization) overseen by the recognized priests of the deity scattered in a number of Ijaw clans. The initiation, according to one of the youth militants I interviewed offers those initiated protection against the gun fire of the Nigerian military[48]. The belief in and the narration of the invincibility of the deity is by no means limited to the youth militants and younger elements of the Ijaw population. On the contrary, it may be more widespread than one would have expected. Actually, another respondent in his early seventies contended:

> The *Egbesu* deity has time and time again assisted the Niger Delta fighters to be more or less invincible in the eyes of the federal government. By making sure that these boys who are defending the livelihood of their fatherland do not lose their lives easily, it has aided the Niger Delta struggle. Do you know that when the *Egbesu* deity dwell in you, that bullets cannot harm you and also machetes cannot cut through your skin. That is our strength against the heavy arms of the military[49].

---

[48] Personal Interview with Ibiam Fiaka in Ekeremor, 14th August 2009
[49] Personal Interview with Elder Elbe, in Nembe, 15th August 2009

This expectation of supernatural protection is akin to a similar phenomenon associated with the former Bakassi Boys and even politicians in the Igbo speaking areas of Nigeria known as "Odeshi" (literally meaning, it does not leak) which refers to supernatural protection against gun shots or bullets and machetes. Just like the case of secret societies, the *Egbesu* initiation involves incantations, scarifications (laying the magic charm inside the skin through a process of rubbing magical portion into the skin freshly cut open by razor blades or other sharp objects) and a strict code of conduct and observances that their contravention results in voiding of the potency of the charm or loss of the bullet proof protection offered by the deity. A similar initiation and a subsequent acquisition of bullet proof magic powers have been noted among the Kamajor fighters in the mid-1990s in Sierra Leone (see, Allie, 2005). However, while the Kamajor fighters can be located to one area of Sierra Leone and operated under a narrower social context, the *Egbesu* deity and practices associated with it are rather more widespread in the vast Ijawland and the initiations are handled by different priests in charge of different cults or shrines of the deity in the different clans though there is the general perception of and acknowledgement of a single high priest of the *Egbesu*.

Different Manifestations of the Occult in the Niger Delta

In the Niger Delta region the recourse to the deity by the youth may be seen as reflective to a reasonable extent of a belief in the rarity of extreme outcomes like death imbued in such beliefs as well as the outcome of frustration with changing the *status quo* through existing means. In other words, the deity is an idiom for facilitating a change of the structure of opportunity in the region for youth population and others. Therefore, Nyamnjoh's (2005) observation regarding the Nyongo among Cameroonians is very instrumental here. In his interesting narration,

Everyday discourses and practices of Cameroonians suggest that witchcraft is about much more than just the dark side of humanity. As a multidimensional phenomenon, witchcraft is best studied as a process in which violent destruction and death are rare and extreme exceptions, employed mostly when all attempts at negotiating conviviality between the familiar and the undomesticated have been exhausted (Nyamnjoh, 2005: 241 – 2).

Witchcraft and occult practices in Africa and elsewhere for that matter are usually shrouded in secrecy, open only to the initiated. Secrecy in this case serves the purpose of mystifying the practice as well as conferring on the initiated superior knowledge, power or wisdom. However, secrecy serves to separate the world of the occult from every day normal lived-in world. In spite of this distinction or difference, there is a basic interrelationship or exchange between the two. Thus, there is a connection of potency in which the world of secret or occult determines or influences events in the normal ordinary world. This connection has been well articulated by the sociologist Georg Simmel (1950) who sees the secrecy as offering the latent possibility of a second world which decisively influences the manifest or everyday world.

As any keen observer of events in the Nigeria Delta would concede the militants often openly declare and demonstrate a faith in the prowess of *Egbesu* (the Ijaw war god)[50]. In this case, it is commonly believed that the deity has the power to confer invincibility on his warriors. However, the reverence of *Egbesu* and the strong belief in it are more widespread than being just limited to the youth militants. In other words, the deity

---

[50] This is actually somewhat of a communal article of faith. For instance one of my research assistants, an Ijaw Kemeaweregha Tebogren while agreeing to assist me in the understanding of the role of *Egbesu* in the Niger Delta struggle warned that there are things about the deity he would never for any price or reason disclose to me (Personal Communication, 28 September 2007).

132

represents a commonality of faith and fate among the Ijaw people. Because it is the god of the people, its invocation by the youth automatically confers community support to their activities. The intertwining of faith and fate which *Egbesu* represents to the various groups in the Ijaw country is perhaps succinctly captured in the observation:

> Egbesu's warrior youth priests are initiated into secret knowledge of 'medicines' conferring immunity to enemy bullets; initiates are supported by 'mothers of the community', by male elders in their customary role of ancestors' representatives, as well as by priests of shrines….(Ifeka, 2006: 723).

Therefore, the alliance of the youth with the *Egbesu* deity apart from belief in its protective and meditative powers[51] is also a route to achieving popular support and shoring up the base of solidarity among different militant groups operating in the region. By so doing the youth bear out a belief that the supernatural endorsement of the gods or other spiritual beings generates a mandate approved by the community (see, Boyer, 2002).

An interesting aspect of the involvement of occult imaginations in the Niger Delta situation is the often unabashed and open manifestation and declarations[52] of strong attachments to such beliefs and symbols by the young people. In other words, one may be tempted to posit that the above implies that the visceral and banal have become pivots of resistance and pursuit of political and economic justice to citizens of the region. The above reality or open declaration of occult allegiance should not

---

[51] In this frame of thought, one of my interviewees contended, "I am an Egbesu soldier, I don't think about dying, I think about victory. I am not afraid at all, we shall win". Personal Interview: Buguma, 3rd September 2009

[52] A common sentiment in this regard is, "I am not just strong, something mightier is behind me. You will not understand but I have a force bigger than whatever the Nigerian government can bring". Personal Interview: Ekeremor 5th June 2009

in any way unnecessarily bother our perceptions even as scholars of modernity. Basically, the expansion of occult and magical practices would seem an expected outcome of the pressures of modernity rather than a contradiction of modernity or more reliably a product of the predictable tension between the allure of modernity and the limits of socio-economic space for a lot of ordinary folks in the developing world including Nigeria. In other words, modernity embodies great promises but spontaneously privilege domination and exploitation which make the negotiation of the promises and good of modernity precarious for ordinary people. Therefore, modernity while in essence holds the promises of abundance, power, privilege and economic largesse for all, the reality has been the enjoyment of these things to the extreme by a few people in postcolonial African societies like Nigeria.

But even more critical and fundamental to any analysis of the relationship between the upsurge in occult imaginations and modernity in Africa is that the lure to acquire these things and their transformation into essential measures of values and social worth has invariably led to the greater urge to indulge in all forms of activities, moral/immoral and legal/illegal in order to access the irrevocable promises of modernity. This has invariably and radically transformed the process of negotiating the occult in a Christianity inundated society like contemporary Nigeria as previously typified in secret and clandestine liaison between an expert or diviner and a client to a more generalized social response to emergencies exemplified by conflict . Along the above frame, the increasing prominence, openness and rampant nature of occult in the modern era may be seen as typifying modernity as a twilight zone between the local/traditional and modern/international. Therefore, as Comaroff and Comaroff (1999) have argued persuasively this implies planes that transcend the here and now, then and there.

Despite the attracting persuasion of the modernity logic espoused above, it is still only one side of the explanation especially since the deployment of the occult in the Niger Delta has not totally conformed to similar incidences in other resource conflict zones in other countries in Africa. Therefore, I see one of the most striking perceptions of the popularity of the *Egbesu* deity among Ijaw youth militants and the rallying point that the deity has become in the conflict as that offered by Gore and Pratten (2003: 233):

> The ideas and practices of the deity Egbesu legitimate and structure the actions its members take within the Niger Delta region. Political commentators and human rights campaigners have commented on Egbesu as a form of spiritual protection for young people resisting the predations of the police and the army, including its reputation to protect an individual from gunfire. However, it is its claims to a precolonial trajectory that rights of ownership over land and resources are defined in opposition to the colonial and subsequent nation state, and these provide a key context for situating counter-narratives to economic marginalization and environmental exploitation.

The above sentiments while revealing the fact that the occult can be invoked as a metaphor for the desire for equity and a rejection of perceived injustice reinforces the stand that occult imaginations even in the context of the infestation of every sphere of life in Nigeria by Christianity does not inherently reflect or represent evil desires. They are rather in this case embodiments and vehicles for achieving the fantasies of a better life in the midst of perceived marginalization or subjugation. A classic case of the misconception of the occult which often bedevils the attempt to understand spirituality and its implications in Africa can found in the signification of an occult related category like witchcraft as inherently evil.

Such definitions which may find support in some quarters these days are basically a-historical and fail to connect witchcraft or occult to other existential realities or cultural universe of the

135

society being studied. A typical case of this practice is found in the contention of Standefer (1970: 32) that a witch is, 'a person who is thought capable of harming others super-naturally through the use of innate mystic power, medicines or familiars, and who is symbolized by inverted characteristics that are a reversal of social and physical norms'. While this definition may find support among later day Pentecostal ministers since it conforms with their doctrine of inherent evil in things they do not understand, it is a classic case of the carry-over of the history of witchcraft in European which has been implanted on the African environment. Therefore, the definition of occult for the benefit of meaningful analysis in the African context calls for more than a dogmatic but unhistorical cognition of social realities in a given society.

While Omeje's (2005a) invocation of the thesis of security re-traditionalisation in explaining the role of the *Egbesu* in the Niger Delta conflict seems rational from a statist perspective, it unfortunately replicates the tendency to see the occult as inherently negative. Thus, it is perceived as an aberration of reality or normality produced from, 'the failure of the state to provide public order and socio-economic development' (Omeje, 2005a: 71). While the above sentiments may capture the Niger Delta conflict in some major respects; the role of the occult in conflict situations deserves a much more different and nuanced approach. Again, the concept of re-traditionalism seems to assume that tradition is a thing of the past and privileging occult practice is a retreat to the past. In other words, the occult should not realistically feature in the modern space in Africa. I am quite sure a reading of writers like Peter Geschiere (1997); Comaroff and Comaroff (1999) and even Ranger (2007) in his apparent bewilderment would persuade us once again to pause and ponder the type of concepts we employ in analyzing the occult.

The inclination towards a statist explanation, in spite of its appeal re-enacts the triumph of meta-narratives over idiographic approaches. Moreover, as earlier argued this approach separates a given belief system or practice from the socio-cultural system of which it is a component (see, Crick, 1979). Evidently the argument that the occult phenomenon is a thing of the past or even its representation as perceived imaginary of only the initiated borders on engagement in denial. In spite of this denial, the occult still exerts great influence in different spheres of society and among diverse groups even till now. Thus, even among the present Edo state of Nigeria, witchdoctors who are known by various local names are registered by the government and provide sundry medical services to the people. Incidentally, these people have recently become demonized by the emergent and rising Pentecostal churches in Edo state as witches who cause evil and encourage idol worship. As Gore and Pratten (2003) state, these people who are seen as witches in Pentecostal imagery paradoxically claim the power to liberate people from witchcraft as do the churches. Despite this, the patronage of such traditional practitioners among many Edo groups is still significant in a society where the idea of black witches who visit innocent people or perceived enemies with evil and other negative afflictions is still dominant.

Egbesu Deity as Motivation in Sustaining Goal Oriented Conflict

The *Egbesu* deity is not just a carry-over of some traditional Ijaw belief system or the mere invocation of a much forgotten past. It is rather a tool with historical roots and evidentiary support that position it as crucial in the contemporary struggle of the Ijaw for improved socio-economic and political rewards or benefits from the Nigerian state. In other words, in spite a noted re-emergence in the 1990s in the context of the conflict in the Ijaw Niger Delta area, the *Egbesu* had existed in the memory of the Ijaw as a god of justice and liberator from external oppression and servitude. The imaginations of the *Egbesu* which reflect the social memory of the Ijaw people can

137

be seen as largely captured in war songs and chants which have been part and parcel of the essential social repertoire of the militants.

One of the critical functions of the *Egbesu* deity for the youth militants as the field data revealed is to motivate them for action and boost their spirits. In this imagination, the act of conflict or warfare begins with a submission to the power of the *Egbesu* which apart from conferring invincibility also induces the right spirit of combat. Perhaps, there is no better way of capturing the above than through a brief examination of the songs and chants of the militants prior to engaging the enemies. Some of these are:

    a. *Muni-muni, fun pele bo eten* (lord –*Egbesu*, cover me with your hands)

    b. *Asawana, wana* (nothing dey happen i.e. you are secured, no problem)

    c. The essence of the *Egbesu* for the war intentions of the Ijaw militants is succinctly captured in one of the popular war songs by the militants. The song goes thus:

Mune mune fun pele bo teri
Yo mune mune fun pele bo teri
Yo Egbesu awou ma mune fun-pele
Ebo-teri yo mune mune fun-pele
Ebo-teri yo

These translate into: *Now we the Egbesu children want to go for war let Egbesu come and cover us with leaves*[53]. This song also provides insight on the belief of the youth militants on the ability of the deity to confer invincibility on them. Therefore:

    d. *Omene teye awouma; omene boi awouma* (we are pure as the eagle – reaffirming the fact that warriors or fighters are innocent.

---

[53] Covering with leaves metaphorically implies making one invisible since the leaves in the jungle makes a soldier blend into the background and become invisible. Even conventional soldiers fighting in jungle employ the green leaves for achieving similar purpose

In other words, the enemies are the aggressors and *Egbesu* as a god of justice is being implored to render judgment in this situation).

e. *Bolou you wou Egbesu*
Bolou you wou Enaiwou ma
Sou doi ya mune
(Go before us *Egbesu*, your children are going to war – affirming that without the deity going to war would be futile)

f. *Gagagubo gagagubo kurowei*
Gagagubo owouye owouye fe
Gagagubo owei
(Song of praise indicating the extra or supernatural being that the Egbesu is i.e. it is captured here as *that which only eats raw things implying a necrophagous and instant ability to devour and consume opponents*)

g. *Agadagba dou yan Egbesu*
Awouma do yan wan biri
Ma tein seboyeme, edenakeme
Emoibaima tarai keme Emo
Baimo erein gbalagbala
(Recognition of the war prowess of the *Egbesu* and *Agadagba* deities; greeting them; followed by the rhetorical question: *the gun you shot last time, how many persons did it kill,* and the response: *three persons in broad daylight i.e. indicating the strength of these deities and their ability to inflict harm on the enemies*)

h. *Ya ya Egbekure Egbe, kure*
Tein ya ofoinpade
Kuro wei bo, ya ya Egbekure (this is a motivational war song used before war to motivate and galvanise the warriors into action and it simply translates into: *No weapon raised against you shall prosper; be it gun, knife or any other and be rest assured that you are always a victor*).

139

The above songs reinforce the thinking that the *Egbesu* as a deity of war and justice has been very useful (psychologically or otherwise) in the struggle of the young people of the Niger Delta. In fact, a respondent captured the above common sentiments among most of the respondents thus, "*Egbesu* lives and the struggle continues. I have been in the battlefield for many times. And you and I know that the federal government only started listening and negotiating with the Niger Delta because of the pressure put on them on the battlefield. I will say there is great progress and there will still be more resistance any time they try to bully anyone around"[54].

There is no doubt that the invocation of the occult or its deployment remains often a vital tool at the local level aspirations towards accessing both power and privilege whether defined as economic or political ascendancy in many African societies. In other words, 'the modernity and relevance of occult belief had crucial, hitherto unnoticed implications on shifting legitimacy and power relations at the local levels of African societies' (Dirk, 2007: 34). Therefore, the occult may be roused to play a mediating role in the quest of people especially at local levels to negotiate valued resources and achieve liberation from perceived socio-economic marginalization as evidenced in the Niger Delta case. It is actually interesting to note that in the case of the Ijaw youth militants, the imagining of the occult represents the wish or desire to reinvent a past where access to resources was strictly determined by local idioms. The Nigerian writer Nonso Okafo commenting on the controversial Okija shrine episode in Anambra state in 2004, sees the reliance on the occult in modern Nigeria as indicating a loss of faith in the formal system established after colonialism (see, Okafo, 2005).

In line with the above, Gore and Pratten (2003) make the apt case of the need to go beyond the premise of re-traditionalism previously privileged by Chabal and Daloz (1999)

---

[54] Personal Interview with Ibiam Fiaka in Ekeremor, 14th August 2009

and vented in connection to the Niger Delta by Omeje (2005a) and address the histories of localized idioms of power, knowledge and accountability which underpin social and popular responses to the instrumentalization of disorder in Nigeria. This approach obviously gives space to both diachronic and synchronic views which are cognizant of the reconfigurations and recombination of popular responses over time.

Chapter Seven

Marginalization and the Re-Invention of the Occult

Marginalization in any political system usually calls attention to the fact that there is both mismanagement of the economy and polarization of socio-economic groups (Adedeji, 1999). On a similar note, Nolutshungu (1996) sees the state as central to marginalization of this kind basically because states preside over diverse and unequal societies and are not always responsive or representative of the interests of all sections of the society. However, it is important to locate marginalisation within the rational action of the state in Nigeria. In this sense, the state in Nigeria during democracy has been accused of using systematic marginalisation to exclude groups that are distant from the locus of power at the centre (see, Anugwom, 2004). Marginalisation, which implies exclusion or alienation from socio-political life, has become largely a politicised concept in Nigeria (Ujomu, 2002) i.e. it has become a theme song of almost all forms of ethno-militant and civil society agitation in Nigeria especially among the Niger Delta groups (see, Anugwom 2004). But probably more germane to the Niger Delta crisis is the contention of Nolutshungu (1996) that marginalization creates vulnerability and is a form of insecurity.

According to Anugwom (2005), the agitation of the ethnic minorities in the Niger Delta has been bolstered by the feeling that the progressive decline in the derivation principle of revenue allocation in Nigeria's fiscal regime has been the product of political and ethnic considerations. It is therefore seen as the outcome of political manipulation by the ethnic majorities in charge of state power. The ironic decline in the derivation principle as revenue from oil increased tremendously since the late 1960s[55] has been captured aptly thus, 'increasingly, states contributed their revenues to a Distributable Pool Account (DPA) at federal level, shared out on the basis of population, need, and other criteria, while the "derivation principle", by which revenues were spent in the geographical area from which they were derived, was downgraded' (Human Rights Watch, 1999: 42). Generally, the whole issue of resources allocation or the distribution of the nation's wealth got mainly from oil among different socio-political groups in Nigeria has been germane to conflict in the country (see, Ujomu, 2002; Danjuma, 1994).

In other words, the literature reveal that ethnic minority crisis and conflict between different ethnic and social groups in the country have been associated one way or the other with Nigeria's federalism and revenue allocation (Adebayo, 1993; Akpan, 1994; Mbanefoh, 1993; Suberu, 2001). The process of revenue allocation in this situation has been fraught with controversy. For the Niger Delta inhabitants, the more vexing issue is what they conceive as the manipulative decline of derivation principle. Thus, there may be a strong linkage between the restiveness of the people and marginalisation and denial of citizenship rights (Anugwom, 2004; Naanen, 1995). Without doubt, the plight of the Niger Delta people and the general nationhood crisis in Nigeria makes an explanation on the parameters of the general notion of the resource curse thesis (see, Auty, 1993; Sachs and Warner, 1995; 2001; Torvik, 2001; van Wijnbergen, 1984 etc.) attractive. In this case, the level of development in the Niger Delta region has been less than commensurate with the perceived resources in the environment. Therefore, the jury is still out on whether the immense oil wealth in the country has been more of a curse than blessing to the people of the Niger Delta.

---

[55] Currently i.e. late 2015 and 2016 oil prices have nose-dived in response to global glut in the oil market. However, many Nigerians optimistically see this as a temporary phase in the country's economic life.

Be that as it may, the Niger Delta conflict typifies the transformation or mutations that play out in a long drawn conflict. The conflict which started from protests and unpredictable struggles in the late 1970s and early 1980s soon snowballed into a massive civil society protest by the 1990s. Anugwom (2007) has seen the hanging of the prominent Ogoni activist Ken Saro-Wiwa by the military junta of the late Sani Abacha in November 1995 as a watershed in the conflict. Besides, he has also pointed out the role of escalating environmental degradation; formidable elite group starting from the late Saro-Wiwa to later activists like Asari-Dokubo and the exposure of the Niger Delta youth through travel to other imaginations of their conditions in the transformation of the conflict from mere civil protest or muffled cry against marginalization to an armed struggle in which local knowledge has facilitated the sustenance of the struggle (Anugwom, 2014). Incidentally, the role of the belief in the occult or *Egbesu* cannot be over-emphasized in the list of the local knowledge repertoire that has sustained the conflict. In other words, the *Egbesu* which is a local manifestation of religious belief and practice has played a prominent role in keeping the spirits of the youth high and emboldening them to face the might of the Nigerian state.

The role of Ken Saro-Wiwa and the MOSOP should also be seen as providing both a defining impetus and enduring transformation of the Niger Delta conflict (see, Anugwom, 2007). In this sense, one sees Ken Saro-Wiwa and MOSOP activism as producing five critical outcomes which fundamentally redefined the conflict thus:

• The internationalization of the conflict especially through tapping into the popular global concern for the environment. In fact, the forced migration or escape of young people from the Niger Delta particularly from the Ogoni to other parts of the world enhanced this process of internationalization and redefinition of the conflict in the youth

145

imagery. The global outcry about environmental degradation in the region also coincided with growing concerns over human rights violation in the region which was a serious issue given that Nigeria then was under one of the most repressive military administrations in its history. In fact, human rights and environmental awareness groups especially the Human Rights Watch (HRW), The Body Shop and Greenpeace were prominent in the campaign. Greenpeace in particular sought to collaborate with the MOSOP in the fight for remediation and protection of the environment.

- The prominence of MOSOP and a perception that the world was beginning to listen to the cries of the Ogoni motivated the involvement of other communities and organizations in the region in the struggle. Even organizations which had been hesitant and timid before drew courage from the Ogoni case.

- The Ogoni Bill of Rights (OBR) which was moved by the MOSOP in October 1990 literally signaled the next phase of the struggle. While the Bill ostensibly captured the grievances and demands of the struggle it equally presaged a resolution to stick with the struggle in spite of the increasing repression from the government. This resolution invariably implied the cognition that a critical change was needed.

- Also, the eventual death of Ken Saro-Wiwa by hanging for the murder of the notable Ogoni four had the effect of forcing a change of tactics from the Ogoni and entire Niger Delta youth who now realized that the stakes were too high for civil protests to win and that the government was determined to extinguish the protests by any means possible.

- Heightened repression by the government and its security agencies culminating in the hanging of the Ogoni Nine; launching of the joint military offensive christened 'operation restore hope' and the use of carrots (mainly monetary inducements) by the government and the TNOCs to break community solidarity and weaken the support base of the struggle through divide and rule strategy

While generally agreeing with the reality of the socio-economic marginalization of the ordinary people in the Niger Delta region, Omeje (2005) in explaining the recourse to the deity by the youth militants averred,

> Outmatched by the military power of their adversaries, these Ijaw groups re-invent and tap into the spiritual power of the ancient Egbesu deity in their homeland, a magical device that complements their limited firepower. Most Ijaw youth fighters are generally believed to be members of the Egbesu cult, and it is widely held that the Egbesu offers magical protection against gunfire to these young militias (Omeje 2005a: 81-82).

But this resembles an ingenious simplification of the reality. In other words, while not intent on rubbishing the capability of the Nigerian armed personnel, the facts remain that: there has not been any real outmatching or clear over-powering of these militant groups by the military[56] that has been operating there since the mid-1990s Ogoni repressions; a fact often attributed to better knowledge of the environment by the militants; actually the only fears among the militants stem from the use of excessive force by the military against old men, women and children as have been witnessed in Ogoni, Choba and Odi at various times since the mid-1990s. Therefore, the idea of outmatching seems exaggerated since the militants have successfully played hide-and-seek with the Nigerian military in that region.

In fact, this may greatly explain the increasing significance accorded to dialogue by the government since 2007. Any militant group that has demobilized so far has done so as the

---

[56] In fact, some observers would argue that the relative peace in the region since 2010 may be the outcome of the amnesty programme initiated by the government in 2009 which was made possible by the impasse in the war between the militants and the JTF of the government.

outcome of negotiations and trade-offs. Equally worth noting here is that the *Egbesu* deity has always been associated with the Ijaw as a symbol of protection, security and often perceived by the Ijaw as having the spiritual powers that could be used in war or conflict situations as evident in the accounts of Omeje himself and even Gore and Pratten (2003). Thus, the deity more or less is deployed whenever and wherever the Ijaw goes to war.

While there are different views on the underlying cause of the Niger Delta conflict, one clear fact remains that years of frustration and disdainful conduct by the government and the TNOCs in the region did not help matters. Cyril Obi seems to capture a prominent strand of this fact thus:

> This is both an expression of frustration as the failure of peaceful protest to lead to any meaningful change in the plight of the people, and anger at the impunity with which the region is being plundered by the state-oil alliance, with the complicity of some local elites and "violent youth" (Obi, 2008: 15).

The reality of widespread and pervasive marginalization and denial of opportunity especially for the younger generation have produced a conflict in which all available arsenal in the environment including religion has been deployed. Without surprise, the narration of marginalization and injustice featured prominently in the views of the people I interviewed. However, these views can be best illustrated with two examples. Thus:

> From the inception if I may use that word, the *Egbesu* deity have always been used to fight for just causes and in this present day there has been and is still great injustice being done to the Niger Delta and when the federal government started using military might to suppress the uprising of the Niger Deltans, the *Egbesu* deity was called upon yet again and it has lived up to expectations. I believe that with the help of the deity to our boys

in the battle field, the federal government came to understand that the solution would not be achieved by force but by negotiation[57].

Also, "the *Egbesu* is our response to the evils of the federal government in Nigeria. With the *Egbesu* no marginalization of the Ijaw would last for long. It is now clear to the government that we are not alone and that we would always fight for what is our own and what has been given to us by God"[58].

While the youth engaged in the conflict have seen recourse to Egbesu and other cult practices as instrumental, the Pentecostal congregations in such Niger Delta cities like Port Harcourt and Yenagoa have sought solace in the enduring kindness of God mediated through his son Jesus Christ. In fact, religious leaders of various faiths in the region have made liberation from suffering and succor in the midst of hardship a core kernel of their messages. This is actually similar to the contention of Gore and Pratten (2003) that while Pentecostal churches demonize the witchcraft of those who are not members, both these other witches and Pentecostal preachers promise the same liberation of people from witchcraft. Therefore, in the crisis of life human beings have found it expedient not only to deploy all available arsenal but even to engage in inventive and innovative usage of what has been in existence including the revival and revision of such phenomena. This tendency is no less true in the wide area of religion where human emotions and fantasies are often granted free reign in the event of life threatening 'tsunamis'.

From the foregoing, it would seem to me that the Niger Delta struggles starting from the pre-civil war actions of the Ijaw youth, Isaac Adaka Boro to the historic struggles of the Ogoni in the 1990s and to the Ijaw sustained conflicts of the late 1990s

---

[57] Personal Interview with Preye Dappa-Silva, 12th August 2009 in Buguma

[58] Personal Interview with a 29 year old ex-militant in Buguma, 12th August 2009.

and 2000s are all efforts at local levels to address perceived and real marginalization of the zone in the socio-political system of Nigeria. The struggle apart from tasking the inventive and creative abilities of the people of the region has also enabled the deployment of all forms of local knowledge and the enriching of perhaps dying idioms of solidarity and group affirmation. Thus, it is pertinent to understand that, 'in Nigeria's southern states youth movements engage in the discourse on marginalization, disorder and crime by drawing on idioms of particularistic community identity and on trajectories of age grades and secret societies' (Gore and Pratten, 2003: 214). The reaching-in as it were to pull out a cultural symbol of power and influence like the *Egbesu* by the Ijaw youth does not only help sustain a peculiar spirit of solidarity for the struggle but equally helps in branding the struggle a typical local liberation and forging a common unassailable element or plank of unity for the separate militant groups in the area. *Egbesu* presents a common front that cannot be voided by the perceived differences in strategies and approaches among the different groups. This may in effect explain the absence of a self-consuming rivalry among the Ijaw of the type that almost aborted the Ogoni project in the 1990s and cost the life of Ken Saro-Wiwa and others (see, Okonta 2008).

Equally important in the understanding of the fact of marginalization and how it plays out in the conflict is the cognition of the youth as a social category that received the greatest impact of the shrinking of local economies and the disruption of traditional local economies of subsistence by ever increasing massive oil exploitation in the region. In this situation, the phase of youth became almost an unending transition of some sort. In framing the youth and their organizations in Nigeria under a 'deep' vertical politics of patrimonialism, Gore and Pratten (2003) came up with the interesting notion of the elongation of youth or 'extended youth'.

The above fact logically creates a robust and critical mass of potential recruits into militant groups. But even more crucial is that it calls attention to the reality that even though socio-economic conditions may be generalized for all groups in the Niger Delta region, it became a most telling experience for the younger generation. Such a situation breeds frustration which generates a loathing for the Nigerian state seen locally as the source of the problem. For the young people of the Niger Delta witnessing an ever increasing and expanding exploitation of oil resources in their environment which ironically is inversely related to opportunities for employment and self-development conjures the transformation of the erstwhile expectant and ambitious youth of yesterday to the youth militant who being dissatisfied with the socio- economic condition of today's Niger Delta youth sees its inversion as signaling the new dawn of fulfilled dreams

Chapter Eight

Making Sense of it All

Occult/Magic as Tool of Conflict

It would appear that young people involved in conflict in Africa in general desire to embrace ritual practices for one reason or another. The above tendency has been noted in the case of the Congo and Liberia for instance (see, Jourdan, 2004; Ellis, 1999). However, while the interpretation of the ritual of inversion of role (for instance male youth dressing like women and fighting in the attire)(see, Ellis, 1999), cannibalism and other disguises adopted by these young soldiers as signaling a transition to adult roles and change of identity (see, Jourdan, 2004) may serve the purpose of the Congo and Liberia cases, the Niger Delta situation is much more complicated and makes reference to a pre-existing religious practice before the onset of conflict. In other words, the belief or practice regarding the *Egbesu* deity in general among the Ijaw of the Niger Delta predates the oil conflict in the Niger Delta region.

In spite of the critical difference pointed out above, the observation by Jourdan (2004) that such practices may puzzle the enemy and create a fear inducing disorientation and conform to the belief that disguises make warriors invincible seems very interesting since the Niger Delta militants equally fight in disguise (covering of faces); though this is not considered by these militants as part of the occult paraphernalia but rather a practical attempt to elude identification. While the covering of faces may serve the practical purpose of concealing one's identity, the wearing of amulets and charms which are common though often covered by the attire may as well be intended to achieve both the aim of instilling fear in the enemy and helping the invincibility of the fighter.

In the already cited study of the involvement of the youth in conflict in North Kivu in the DR. Congo, Jourdan (2004) also sees the effect of historical dynamics connected to erosion of traditional system of land distribution which led to the progressive socio-economic marginalization of the younger generations as providing a robust population of youth eager to enroll in the war in the country as militias. The above observation is indeed instructive for the case of the Niger Delta where the equivalent of erosion of traditional system can be perceived in the massive oil exploitation in the region in the last five decades that has blighted traditional ecology and livelihood systems. This situation has been compounded by years of general neglect by the government which has produced a frustrated and eager to fight youth population. Therefore, youth while often seen as possessed of uncritical courage and daring, only exhibit these when confronted with dire socio-economic or life threatening situations that help a definition of courage as the ability to confront these problems or their sources head-on. As Jourdan (2004) aptly contends, violence then assumes a political value and its practice constitutes one of the rare alternatives to social marginalization.

Probably, the best way of dealing with the occult in modern Africa especially in relation to its negative deployment and the violence associated with its imageries (witchcraft violence/witch hunts) is not to engage in denial or shelter under the dubious notion of a recalcitrant but antithetical past but rather to first come to terms with its reality and manifold nature. As Dirk (2007) argues, occult or witchcraft is not just current and affecting relevant aspects of life in sub-Saharan Africa but also has impact on actual social, economic and political structures. Perhaps, it would be necessary to state here that the nature of impact meant is necessarily not in the form of a Harry Potter like magical wand that blows into reality human beings, wakes the dead, or automatically turns election results in the favour of the most obscure candidate who despite unpopularity with the electorates commands the most potent witchcraft power; but may be seen in the sense of how imageries of the occult; the fear it generates; the anxiety it sponsors and the security or power imbued in it affect the course of actions of individuals or groups in the society whether in the economic realm, social relations, or political spheres.

Occult, the Modern State and Underdevelopment

The upsurge in popularity of youth militant action and response (to perceived shortcoming on the part of government or the political class) in Nigeria and elsewhere in Africa may be related one way or another to the failure of the state to protect or provide for its citizens. Harnischfeger (2006) has related the rise in militant associations in modern Nigeria to the failure of the state. Thus, in the Niger Delta the deployment of the occult in the conflict can be rationalized on the grounds of the failure of the government to effectively settle the grievances of the oil bearing communities in the region. It is in this way akin to the tendency to result to occult forces when there is no effective mechanism to resolve a given conflict (see, Harnischfeger, 2006). In the case of the Niger Delta youth, the *Egbesu* is a symbol of justice which has been called into service as a result of the failure of the Nigerian state to address the perceived injustice in the oil exploitation regime in the country. However, it would seem that the failure of the state which makes possible the recourse to militant action equally implies in the broader sense dissatisfaction with the project of modernity.

In this case, militant groups often dig deep into the traditional cultural elements of the people in the bid to achieve legitimacy and offer a countervailing traditional alternative to the modern state and its apparatus of civil order. In addition, these groups are often cast as providing popular options to the failure of the formal institutions as agencies for actualizing individual and group aspirations. One outcome of the above may be seen as the increasing popularity of the occult as vehicle of creating belief and reliability by these groups. But the above do not just imply a novel process of re-traditionalism as some writers[59] would have us believe. My grouse with the idea of re-traditionalism is that it ultimately may suggest a time gap in which occult beliefs and practices became extinct only to materialize again as the state building project faltered. Far from this, the occult has always been around but may have acquired more impetus with the faltering or incapacity of the modern state. Henrietta Moore and Todd Sanders capture a part of my own stance here when they argued:

> Contemporary witchcraft, occult practices, magic and enchantments are neither a return to 'traditional' practices nor a sign of backwardness or lack of progress; they are instead thoroughly modern manifestations of uncertainties, moral disquiet and unequal rewards and aspirations in the contemporary moment (Moore and Sanders, 2001: 3).

But beyond the above sentiments, the case of the Niger Delta especially when viewed in relation to the massive environmental mayhem which oil exploitation has caused in the region borders equally on the question of rights. In other words, central to the conflict in the region is the determination of the ordinary citizens to fight the government and its agents infringing on their right to safe habitation and livelihood in their environment (see Anugwom, 2007). In this sense, the struggle of the militants becomes more or less a last ditch action against the impairment of the rights of the people and for which the occult becomes as much necessary as any other viable

---

[59] Omeje (2005a) is typical of this; and even Harnischfeger's (2006) interesting article on "State Decline and the Return of Occult Powers: the case of Prophet Eddy in Nigeria" veers towards this belief in re-traditionalism

indigenous resource deployable in order to achieve the goals of the struggle which are built essentially on a refutation and contestation of the project of modernity as presently constituted in Nigeria. In this regard, one finds the replication of the Niger Delta conflict which typifies a growing disenchantment and rejection of the *status quo* in various degrees and guises in other parts of Nigeria. But beyond a mere rebuttal of modernization or the fleeting desire for a return to the idyllic African past is the derailment of the project of modernity in the country. Therefore:

> My impression is that state-centered modernization indeed went hand in hand with a process of disenchantment. Yet in the last decades of the twentieth century, major achievements of modernization were lost. Life has become so insecure, even in rural areas that people must submit to the patronage of more powerful groups or individuals. Without protection by local politicians or militias, by secret cults or religious communities, individuals would be largely without rights, since rights only exist if they can be defended by force (Harnischfeger, 2006: 68).

There is a reality in the Nigerian context which suggests that the involvement of the youth in occult practices may be equally reflective of the recourse to this tool by the older members of the society and key personages in political life. In this sense, occultism especially its negative deployment is often a strong tool in the arsenal of the political class in Nigeria. In fact, as was reported in the *Tell Magazine*, a former Nigerian leader who died while in office, Sani Abacha was popularly known for surrounding himself with all manner of purveyors of occult powers and sorcerers (see, Tell Magazine, March 25, 1996 pp. 8). In the face of the above, the perception that confronting the political class head-on as the Niger Delta militants did requires the possession of a higher power may have been privileged and sustained.

It would amount to gross a-historicism to argue that occultism is peculiarly African or even largely a developing world phenomenon. Thus, examining the upsurge of occult practices in the 19th Century London society for instance, Pile (2006) has argued that occultism was thoroughly modern, and attempted to provide holistic understanding of the universe that included both scientific and spiritual dimensions. The scholar Alex Owen (1989; 2004) has done a very good job of capturing the enchantment of the Victorian age England with various forms of occult practices and beliefs. Even more insightful is that Owen records how some occult formations like the Theosophical Society migrated from one western domain (New York) to another (London) and the blurred line between the scientific and the occult. In the late Victorian age England occult practice was more a vocation of the elites than the less privileged members of the society and in the cocoons of these elite occult societies, people were preoccupied with a wide range of metaphysical issues ranging from the popular astral travel, divination to the more enticing science of alchemy and invocation of spirits and spirit mediums.

But the occult in the above situations were ostensibly dressed as tools of improving society through improving man's knowledge of the unknown and as such similar, if not the same as science. Occult when used in this sense or even expressed as a positive tool resembles some form of science. Without doubt even the most eccentric occult in the Western world of the pre-20th Century era seemed webbed one way or the other into science. The case of the legendary Dr. John Dee of the English Elizabethan era is testimony to the above thinking. As has been recounted by Steve Pile:

> Dr. Dee was indeed a scientist, but his version of science was indistinguishable from what might now be thought of as being magic – yet it also bears a striking resemblance to Victorian occult practices, with its similar use of mystical Christianity, natural

philosophy, astral observation and alchemical experimentation. Just as the Victorians were trying to make contact with spirits in the other world through séances, so Dee was attempting to talk to angels. Dr Dee's alchemistry and conversations with angels cannot be so easily set apart from mathematics and navigation (Pile, 2006: 313-314).

Pile goes on to clarify the nature of the occultism of the modern urban Victorian age by making the instructive observation that only in the mechanical models of the universe could science be distinguished from magic or spiritual accounts of the universe. In his own words,

> In other models of the universe including those grounded in observational or positivistic experimental science, there was far less to distinguish matter from spirit, science from the occult. Indeed, although they are now usually assumed to be entirely different, there are more links between scientific and occult cosmological models than many would care to admit (Pile, 2006: 314).

It actually does not take much convincing to believe that the West even till now is still the domain of esoteric and pseudo-knowledge pursuits that are basically occult oriented. In most major cities in the West especially in London and New York, the painstaking observer would notice the practice of different forms of the above new magic in the form of such things as séances/spirit medium, psychic fayres, palm reading, Wicca, spiritual home circles and even new age philosophy and unorthodox group prayers etc. Thus, the spectral is as much a characteristic of the developing world as it is of these Western urban towns.

Perhaps, the only major difference between the occult of the West and that of contemporary Africa is that while the development of precise science and formal state institutions now bridge the needs and desires for occult in popular culture in the developed world, the incapacity of social and formal institutions especially in providing for and protecting citizens generate the opposite effect of upsurge in occult practices in the developing world. Hence, one agrees with the contention that, 'far from magic dying out in the modern Western city, magic is thriving. Indeed I would argue, it is a strangely normal part of the daily life of Western cities' (Pile, 2006: 316).

The Youth, Conflict and Occult

While there is obviously fascinating logic in the contention that, 'witchcraft offers hidden means to grab power, but at the same time it reflects sharp feelings of impotence; it serves especially to hide the sources of power' (Geschiere, 1997: 9); one cannot help indicate that while in the case of the Niger Delta, the idea of feeling impotent may exist there is no doubt that the recourse to *Egbesu* deity reflects equally the tensions and pressures of coming to terms with one's lived experiences. In this sense, it is only reasonable to believe that the *Egbesu* belief apart from the assumed invincibility it generates among the youth militants may also reflect both the urge in these young people to generate courage in themselves and more critically generate terror in others that may prove beneficial to their cause. In other words, the invocation of the deity is seen by the militants as a way of generating terror in the opposition and affecting the outcome of the conflict one way or another. Incidentally terror even though largely a psychological tool has been seen as having a tactical function in terms of acting as substitute for lack of adequate and superior weapon and in affecting the course of the war to the advantage of the terror-bearer (see, Jourdan, 2004).

Beneduce et al (2006) in examining the involvement of youth engaged in conflict with the occult contend that young recruits are in many cases responsible for the atrocious and violent acts of violence which are often macabre and ritualized. These young people are thus seen by their communities as 'witches' or 'polluted men' and thus represent a danger for the whole community (Beneduce, et al, 2006). But while the rituals and predisposition to the occult which mark youth combatants in the Congo can also be seen among the Niger Delta youth militants, the widely reported cases of utilization of extreme terror, rape, torture and cannibalism reported in the Congo case (see, Beneduce et al, 2006; Jourdan, 2004) were not in any significant sense replicated in the Niger Delta conflict. Though one can argue that the Congo war is an example of a high intensity conflict while the Niger Delta conflict is assumed to be a low intensity conflict.

My investigations reveal that there was quite a good number of the case of the wrongful employment of the powers of *Egbesu* by the youth militants. Thus, "the *Egbesu* deity is and would have been even more effective if it was managed properly. Those in charge obviously used it to their own advantage as they enriched themselves and became warlords" [60]. This was as much acknowledged as it was thought of as not in any significant sense vitiating the influence of the deity. As a result, "the *Egbesu* deity will continue to protect the Ijaw kingdom and its people irrespective of other people's perception about the deity. Some people believe that *Egbesu* deity has not been fair in distribution of justice since some of its worshippers like the militants use it for their selfish aggrandizement and interests"[61]. In other words, the infractions in the use of the deity do not detract from the powers of the deity since it is seen as equal to the task of disciplining those who go contrary to its rules and precedents. Hence, one of my respondents argued:

---

[60] Personal Interview with Godbless Miebi in Kaiama, 12th August 2009
[61] Personal Interview with Moses Siloko Siasia in Grand Brass, 11th August 2009

The *Egbesu* deity has been accused of several misconducts of its former members, and this is because some bad eggs that got the protection of the deity started using it for purposes other than the Niger Delta struggle. But be rest assured that the *Egbesu* deity always fights for itself. Anyone that is guilty cannot live with the *Egbesu* spirit because the spirit will end that soul[62].

But in employing the occult, the youth also seek some macabre rewriting of the scripts of their lives. The youth as a social group even in the midst of conflict do not stand alone but rather engage in interchange or exchange with the other sections of the society. The actions of the youth especially in conflict have impact on the social rubric of the society that is often more far-reaching than expected. Therefore, one thing which the analysis of the youth militant driven Niger Delta conflict has often over-looked is the effect of conflict in recreating and reshaping both the normative patterns of the region and set of cultural reference point and social opportunities for different segments of the society. In responding violently to the socio-economic 'terror' unleashed on the oil communities by the government and international oil capital the conflict impacts enduringly on people's cultural frame of reference and the framing of opportunities and access to them by the youth population. This is akin to the contention of Beneduce et al (2006) in reference to the war in the Congo that conflict reshapes the structure of opportunity and meaning at the level of grassroots interaction.

Long running conflicts dependent on youth often reshape communities not only in terms of cultural meanings and opportunities but more critically entails a shift in generational role definitions. As the Niger Delta conflict shows both novel redefinition and redeployment of the role of the supernatural

---

[62] Personal Interview with Preye Dappa-Silva in Buguma, 12th August 2009

which even though anchored on popular symbols (which are necessary to mediate grassroots support) reflect new cultural frame of reference significantly different from the ideal. Equally critical is the redefinition of virtues and access to socio-economic opportunity. For instance there may be new definitions of authority, power and status in the communities.

Reconstructing the Youth in the age of Conflict in Africa: Major Concerns

It is important to appreciate the nature and the socio-environmental factors which mediate youth as a social category and imbue it with the potentials of agency often lurking at the edge of violence and force. Youth is an acute repository of influence and a site of constant re-imagining and re-modification of observed and perceived socio-political currents and events. Therefore, 'youth is a complex, fluid and permeable category which is historically and socially situated. As such it is a site for particular and localized framings of human agency constituted by various intersecting and contested discourses' (Gore and Pratten, 2003: 215).

There is obviously no gainsaying the fact that the Niger Delta conflict much like similar conflicts in the West African region (Liberia, Sierra Leone) has received impetus from the youth population. In other words, the youth in the Niger Delta have formed a critical mass for recruitment and involvement in the conflict in the region. While the youth population may be seen universally as sharing certain common attributes or tendencies like assertiveness, impulsive action, courage (often mixed with little caution), stamina (physical and mental strength) among others which easily make them amenable to conflict there is need also to see youth as a social category which is amenable to the socio-cultural or normative patterns of a given society.

In the case of the Niger Delta and some other communities in Africa, the youth are culturally seen as belonging to the rank of warriors and soldiers or the defenders of the integrity of their communities (see, Anugwom, 2007). In a typical division of labour, the older members of the population provide analytical and advisory context of situations and the youth enforce the outcome of these or act as the foot soldiers of their community. In this sense, though the youth act even in conflict, such actions and directions of action are affected by the imaginations of significant others. In contemporary times, the significant others may in some cases equally be those who manipulate the youth in conflict situations.

As Hutchful and Aning (2004: 207) argue, 'though much emphasis is often placed on the agency and autonomy of youth as political actors, they are also open to manipulation by other groups in society'. Thus, manipulation may be used in getting the youth to both start and sustain conflict, not even by the usual community elders or leaders of thought representing common interests but also by others pursuing selfish individual interests within and beyond the community or social group. Even in a large geographical scope, the force of manipulation functions and often exacts more influence though sometimes concealed and veiled more than any other consideration.

Related to the above is the incontrovertible fact that the youth in the Niger Delta have also been unwittingly exploited by the political elites in the region. Hence, the complicity of the political class in the Niger Delta conflict has been proved beyond reasonable doubt with the involvement of some militants in the realization of the political ambitions of state governors in the region. Actually, two of the most popular of the militants, Mujaheed Asari-Dokubo and the Okrika warlord Ateke Tom were at one time or another the protégés of a prominent state governor in the region and were influential in garnering electoral victories probably through intimidation and terror in the 1999 and 2003 general elections in Nigeria (see, Best and von Kemedi, 2005; HRW, 2005 etc.). At some point militant factions loyal to Dokubo were engaged in conflict with those of

Ateke Tom. A crisis resulting from allegations in popular myth that Ateke Tom displaced Dokubo as the right hand man of the governor.

This displacement is often seen as the reason why Dokubo took up violent armed protest against the Nigerian state and oil corporations. In other words, this turned him from embarking on peaceful struggle to violent struggle obviously utilizing the money garnered during the elections to procure needed materials for his group of militants. However, it must be mentioned that Dokubo's utility to the politicians in the first place must have emanated from a good knowledge of the use of violence or physical harassment and intimidation of opponents, so losing out in the camp of the governor did not really turn him violent but rather may have given a more vicious and an anti-establishment angle to this predisposition in him. Be that as it may, there is evidence in the foregoing discourse that violence has dynamism of its own and actually breeds shifting alliances and transitory networks liable to change and recombination even without notice.

Even though the extant literature on the Niger Delta conflict have looked at the militants more or less as some group of freedom fighters with a just cause (see, Okonta, 2006; 2008 for example), it may also be fruitful to examine the personal motives which often make the youth eager receptors of conflict. Apart from the simplified notion of conflict as subterfuge for economic mode of negotiating modernity which neglects the fact that armed conflict can equally be seen as negotiating death and thus irrational in some respects; there is need to look at the personal motives which predispose the youth to violent conflict. As Jourdan (2004: 162) argues, 'young combatants use violence to their own profit, in order to renegotiate and improve their social status. In this sense, violent practices have a political value because they manifest a will to undermine the social order, promoting at the same time new forms of organization'. Though Jourdan argues above with specific reference to the Congo war,

I see broad similarities or rather its possibilities in the Niger Delta conflict. The perception of the personal motives of young combatants or youth involved in conflict goes a long way in appreciating the seeming endless nature of such conflicts. Basically, ending the conflict would imply that the youth lose the opportunity to impose their subjectivities which the conflict offers and succumb to the *status quo ante* of social organization where adults are usually in the driving seat and determine the direction of the society as well as the access and control of valuable resources in the society.

Chapter Nine

Some Encouraging Conclusions?

The Why and How of the Conflict

Perhaps a good but inverse way of ending our discourse so far is to try a brief re-cap of the entire conflict in the oil producing Niger Delta of Nigeria. This exercise which I hope to keep brief would surely inform our understanding of the dynamics of the conflict and the eventual role of the occult in the conflict. In a clear chronological order, the Niger Delta oil conflict can be seen as originating from the daring action of the late Isaac Adaka Boro in February 1966. It was the then young Isaac Boro who as an undergraduate student of the University of Nigeria Nsukka led other Ijaw youth in the Niger Delta to form the original Niger Delta Volunteer Force (NDVF) and staged an abortive and largely unarticulated attempt to establish a Niger Delta Republic. The attempt even though borne out of the need of the Niger Delta people to secure their resources from their immediate neighbours – the Igbo who they saw as predators under the short-lived and tragically ended regime of General T.T Umunnakwe Aguiyi-Ironsi led federal government in 1966 was also the beginning of the often undisguised separatism which has underlined the Niger Delta conflict through time.

Be that as it may, the Boro uprising and the soft campaign mounted through the media and public forums in the late 1970s and early 1980s by such Niger Delta elites as Melford Okilo may be signaled as the origin and first stages of the conflict respectively. However, these two stages were later transformed into a more radical, articulate and widespread campaign in the 1990s by a couple of factors including mainly the increased centralization and control of oil revenues by the federal government or the prominence of fiscal centralism (see, Anugwom, 2005); the obvious stupendous wealth in the black gold as evidenced by the oil boom of the 1970s and consequent upon this, the increased pace and spread of oil exploitation reminiscent of a scramble for the oil resources in the region.

As already indicated the second stage of the Niger Delta struggle can be denoted as much more vibrant, radical, articulate and widespread geographically. The transformation of the struggle in the 1990s to the above level owned largely to both the role of the late Ken Saro-Wiwa led MOSOP and the personal commitment of Saro-Wiwa himself to the struggle. Perhaps the change of gears was robustly shown with the presentation of the popular Ogoni Bill of Rights (OBR) by the MOSOP to the federal government in October 1990 soon after the formation of the MOSOP[63] (in September 1990) demanding autonomy for the region and control of the oil resources in the region. However, Saro-Wiwa's tenacity of purpose in actualizing these demands and use of experience acquired as a writer and creative artist to drum up both support for the MOSOP and exposure of the devastation of oil exploitation on the communities of the Niger Delta typified largely by his attack on Anglo-Dutch oil giant Shell brought the Niger Delta situation to the forefront of international development discourse and changed the course of events.

The death by hanging of Ken Saro-Wiwa in November 1995 presaged the third stage of the conflict which can be

---

[63] In tracing the development of the MOSOP, Okonta (2008) characterizes it as a mass-based social organization that embraced the path of peaceful protest to demand the economic and political autonomy of the Ogoni; payment of compensation by Shell and the Nigerian government for both pollution of the Ogoni farmlands and fishing streams and the oil taken from the land since 1958 when commercial exploitation of oil commenced. These demands were embodied in the popular Ogoni Bill of Rights (OBR) forwarded to the government in October 1990. However the government in typical misreading and adoption of the right is might attitude that helped in complicating the Niger Delta crisis responded by dispatching armed soldiers to Ogoni in mid-1993 (see, Okonta, 2008).

characterized as violent and anchored by the youth. Thus, the third stage of the struggle started from 1997/8 when Ijaw youth still reeling from the unprecedented repression of the government amply demonstrated by the hanging of Saro-Wiwa took on the mantle of leadership of the struggle. The ideals of these youth were contained in the 1998 Kaimaa Declaration issued by the Ijaw Youth Council (IYC) which was also formed that year.

In addition to the above, one may still talk about the fourth stage of the struggle which signaled the loss of coordination and total control by the IYC of the Ijaw youth and youth of other ethnic groups in the region. This stage was the stage of incomparable violence, kidnapping and destruction of oil installations and facilities championed by a plethora of youth militant organizations. It would be in order to point out that this stage which derived great impetus from the senseless massacre of civilians by the Nigerian army in the Bayelsa town of Odi in November 1999 (the Odi massacre) was monumental in that it came only a few months into the tenure of the new democratic government led by Olusegun Obasanjo and which on its inauguration in May that year had promised to make the Niger Delta problem a key thrust of the administration's policies. Also, the destruction was massive since according to the Human Rights Watch (1999) all buildings in the town apart from the Bank, the Anglican Church and the community health centre were destroyed and burnt to the ground.

In an article in the Pambazuka News the Head of Nigeria based Environmental Rights Action, Nnimo Bassey (Bassey, 2006) puts the number of people killed in the attack by Nigerian soldiers at 2500. The attack was a reprisal action for the killing of twelve policemen by criminal miscreants near the town. This massacre which followed on the heels of the re-entry of democracy in Nigeria eventually produced environment seasoned Niger Delta youth fighters like Asari-Dokubo and Ateke Tom. Perhaps, the pinnacle in using violence as a tool of the struggle was reached with the emergence of the MEND, a loose coalition of different militant organizations in the region. The MEND waged what may be seen as the most violent and relentless armed struggle on the oil industry displaying extraordinary courage, bravery and daring of security operatives.

These attributes of the MEND and the elusive nature of the group have also privileged the narrative of the occult. However, the invocation of the occult has been in existence right from the onset of the conflict and is even a common attribute of armed conflict in most traditional societies in Nigeria. The high use of amulets, charms and invocation of the *Egbesu* deity by the MEND fighters has meant imaginations of some connection between occult practice and the resilience of these fighters.

Regarding the MEND and the threat it constitutes, Obi (2008: 18) argued:

> For now the most potent militant group engaging in local resistance but targeting a global audience is the Movement for the Emancipation of the Niger Delta (MEND). MEND has launched daring raids into fortified oil installations onshore and offshore and kidnapped foreign oil workers, detonated explosive devices near oil compounds, and fought pitched battles on land and at sea with Nigeria's military forces, and publicized its activities on various global media (Obi, 2008: 16).

However, the MEND even though reflecting a loosely organized confederation of armed groups in the Niger Delta has commanded more attention and generated more terror and dread than all other Niger Delta militant groups before it. The conviction of the government that the group can actually bring the oil industry to a collapse witnessed by the dwindling revenue from oil during its hey days between late 2008 and early 2009 must have forced the hands of the federal government in both establishing the Ministry of the Niger Delta and coming out with the initial ₦50 billion Niger Delta Amnesty program in 2009.

The ability of the group to successfully strike deep oil installations and the daring attack on the Atlas Cove Jetty in Lagos were fundamental testaments to its prowess[64]. Also, the attack in Lagos revealed the vulnerability of oil installations and the inability of security agencies to put a stop to the activities of the group. Possibly, the Lagos attack which seemed totally senseless then was meant to buttress the often repeated claim of the MEND that it can launch attack anywhere in the country[65].

The MEND in spite of its reliance on terror is probably the group which has been most open to the media and interest groups on its activities. According to Junger (2007), the group employs the internet to send mails to the outside world and even

---

[64] The Atlas Cove attack in Lagos by MEND occurred in July 2009; the attack in lagos was at a docking station over 250 miles from MEND's heartland in the Niger Delta. The attack resulted in a reduction of Nigeria's oil production by over 20% and had deleterious effect on the oil mono-economy of Nigeria. It was also a watershed in youth militant violence in Nigeria since it showed that the MEND had the capacity and courage to strike anywhere in Nigeria. Perhaps, this was the last straw in the proverbial camel's back that made the amnesty programme inevitable from the perspective of the government.

[65] It is important to note that two actions of the MEND between 2008 and 2009 stood out in causing jittery in government circles and forcing government to finally change approach. These actions were the bombing of the Shell Bonga oil platform laying about 120 kilometres from the Niger Delta coast line in June 2008 and the bombing of the 50 million litre capacity Atlas Cove Jetty in Lagos on July 12 2009. The attack on the Bonga oil platform led to its shutting down immediately by Shell and meant the loss of about 10 per cent of Nigeria's oil production. The expensive Bonga oil platform which is situated at a considerable distance from the shorelines was proof of the ability of the MEND to attack all of Nigeria's oil installations. The audacious bombing of the Atlas Cove jetty in Lagos attracted much public outcry. In responding to the attack the popular Nigerian Daily, the Daily Independence (2009) in an editorial saw it as malicious, rascally and provocative; it also further argued that by the attack the MEND overstepped its boundary and runs the risk of frittering away the immense goodwill it has gathered among the Nigerian populace for its struggle. In spite of the fact that these actions especially the Lagos Atlas Cove bombing were heavily criticized they both underline the capacity of the MEND and in my view served unequivocal notice to the government on the inevitability of dialoguing with the group or its leaders.

takes journalists to its camps in the swamp of the Niger Delta. This posture contradicts the ultra-secretiveness of similar organizations before it in the region. The willingness to dialogue and engage in exchange with neutral parties must have won it credibility as a focused rebel group. But beyond the above, these attributes made it possible for it to succeed in generating attention and sustaining the focus of the world on activities in the region. However, the downside of the group is the emergence of rampant kidnappings in the region. While the organization protests that it is not involved in kidnapping for ransom in the region, its activities including kidnapping of expat oil workers to make its point must have certainly provided the cover and insecurity exploited by other criminal youth gangs and bandits in the region for their various nefarious activities.

Reality, Psychology or What?

Without doubt some of what passes as occult manifestations in modern Africa may be domiciled in the realm of popular culture narratives (especially folklore; rumours; hear-say; anecdotes etc.). But even such narratives as Geschiere (1997) shows may be a product of the existential reality of the people or their attempt to find expression for sudden change in fortune or express consternation over social oppression or opportunism. In this sense, people may result to 'mouthing' the occult when they find out that the political and economic power or privilege is either opaque or outrageously unjust and irrational. The occult becomes not just an explanation but rather the expression of frustration, consternation and dispiritedness at the way modern society works. Therefore, the occult occupies the nether region between reality and the psychological needs of the individual to achieve some balance with his environment or comprehend events in the environment.

Be that as it may, one of the key challenges to the imagination for some time was how the Niger Delta militants could afford the large and extensive armoury at their disposal. Apart from the internal role of capitalist opportunists in the bunkering business (see, Kemedi, 2006) and the political class; there is need to understand that oil which can be seen as an unlootable resource travels a long distance in pipelines which according to Ross (2003) offers the militants an unceasing flow of extortion opportunities. In this way, un-lootable resource like oil in the case of Nigeria provides a source of finance for militants which helped prolong the conflict. Equally crucial and ironically creative in the Niger Delta case is that the kidnapping of expat workers have been exploited for funding the operations of the militant groups.

In spite of the abundance of narratives and practices supportive of the occult imagery in the oil conflict in the Niger Delta of Nigeria, one cannot help seeing evidence or better still the imperative of the psychological realm here. In this sense, since the youth militants still died from the bullets of the Joint Military Task Force (operation restore hope) and were often apprehended by these security operatives in spite of what appears to be an over-domination of occult beliefs and practices, then the thinking is that the recourse to *Egbesu* serves a major role in endowing courage and privileging obtuse resistance in the militants. Perhaps, the use of *Egbesu* by the youth militants in the Niger Delta resembles the scenario among the Maka of Eastern Cameroon where in spite of perceived disturbing effects, occult forces are used constructively to protect oneself or reinforce one's authority and desire to succeed in life (see, Geschiere, 1997).

While the belief in invincibility and protection offered by the deity are of critical psychological value to the youth militants, quite a lot of the respondents make a persuasive submission on the real value of the deity in the conflict. Therefore,

> Like I said earlier, the Egbesu deity has been of immense support to the Ijaws who are also a large number of the Niger

173

Deltans. The Egbesu deity gave spiritual support to our boys that before now, the Nigerian army thought that it would crush the Niger Delta struggle by military force, but they were disappointed because the fight continued and there is no doubt that the struggle has brought about many changes and development in the Niger Delta, and there is still hope that the present 13% derivation would be reviewed upwards so the Egbesu have had a good effect on the Niger Delta struggle[66].

This impact is even perceived as going beyond the Niger Delta since, "different groups have made their voices heard not only in Nigeria but internationally because of the force *Egbesu* deity has put in them. These voices have brought attention to the Niger Delta region and there is no doubt that more and more attention is now been given to the region. We know that with more attention given to the Niger Delta region, that in little or no time, it can measure up to the standards of all other oil rich regions of the world" [67]. In other words, the deity was instrumental to whatever success that the conflict has achieved for the people of the Niger Delta. For a former militant who would rather remain anonymous, "I believe that the support of the *Egbesu* has been very powerful. To fight against soldiers, people who are trained to fight is not easy but we try and the *Egbesu* gives us both power and courage to carry on. It is not easy my brother"[68].

The foregoing supports the orientation that in addition to a marked dynamism of beliefs in the supernatural or occult there is evidence that such beliefs are either produced or reinforced by insecurity and unpredictability. Therefore, as it were for the

---

[66] Personal Interview with Monday Odion, Nembe, 17th August 2009

[67] Personal Interview with Chief Akuro Diette – Spiff in Grand Brass, 10th August 2009

[68] Personal Interview with a middle aged former militant in Ekeremor, 19th August 2009.

inhabitants of the Trobriand Islands of Malinouski, it may be for the youth militants in the Niger delta.

Understanding Occult and Resolving Conflicts

The challenge of the Niger Delta conflict should be seen as going beyond the mere cessation of hostilities. In this case, the conflict has generated different effects on the communities in the region especially in view of the involvement of the youth. It is only reasonable to believe that the involvement of the youth militants would affect the social fabric and status ordering in a society in which authority is mediated essentially through age. In other words, the conflict may have created social problems bordering on new roles for the youth and the relationship between different age groups (extremely typified as young and old) in the rural communities of the Niger Delta. Apart from challenges regarding how to integrate a young person who had previously acquired and impudently exercised the roles of the adult during conflict into the ideal social structure where there is a direct relationship between age and access to power and authority; there is also the question of opportunities for actualization of aspirations that should be the prerogative of every young person. In this sense, one needs to understand that, "a child who exercises violence against an adult not only goes beyond his social role but also even inverts it" (Beneduce et al, 2006: 36). The above sentiments point at a significant aspect of post-conflict peace building challenges that gnaws at the heart of the social order and the wholesome emergence of society from conflict.

A debilitating factor which has undermined actions by the government and the TNOC's to address the Niger Delta problem including the recent 2009 Amnesty deal is the alluring tendency to succumb to a mono-causal mode in explaining the conflict and adopting amelioration methods or solutions to the conflict. In other words, the Niger Delta conflict just like any other long drawn conflict elsewhere is both complex and multi-dimensional and thus demands solutions that are anchored on this understanding. At this point, it would be instructive to understand that:

> As conflicts unfold and mutate, so do the mutations and relationships underpinning them. Monocausal explanations of conflicts may be deceptively attractive or persuasive due to their apparent simplicity, but they are ultimately unhelpful. Conflicts must be understood on the basis of multiple and complex causes" (Hutchful and Aning, 2004: 200).

While the above calls attention to the danger of unduly relying on mono-causal explanation and building a solution on that as implied in Collier's (2000) economic model, it does not automatically nullify the economic agenda in its totality even in the Niger Delta conflict since the economic dimension has been equally as consistent as the issue of grievance arising from socio-economic marginalization and environmental degradation among others in the conflict through the years. The popular war cry "resource control" in the Niger Delta underpins the importance of economic considerations in addition to others in the conflict. Despite the above, over-emphasizing the economic motive to the disregard of the other factors may be counter-productive and generate solutions that are anchored on the mindset that peace can be bought.

As Beneduce et al (2006) argue for any attempt at peace to be successful in a conflict area there is need to take cognizance of both the motivations of the individual perpetrators and the social transformation which occurs in a society as a result of protracted use of violence. While the Niger Delta conflict is not exactly that of the Congo that Beneduce and his colleagues studied, the value of the above observations should not be lost on peace attempts in the region. It is in recognition of the above that the 2009 amnesty programme of the Yar'Adua government seems not yet the final solution. So far, the posturing and utterances of key government officials involved in the programme reflect an elitist 'othering' approach that is scantly aware of either the individual motives of the key actors in the militant organizations or the different dimensions of the impact on the various rural communities which served as either the operational bases of the militants or the theatres of the violent confrontation between the youth militants and security forces. For instance, the issue of displacement or dispersion of communities and individuals in these communities were hardly factored into the programme as well as the impact of the violence on the cultural frame of reference in these places and the critical effect of the conflict on local livelihoods.

Without doubt there have been severe criticisms of the amnesty programme especially in terms of its execution and outcomes even after five years. According to Ibaba (2011) the amnesty program does not critically address what has been labeled the frustration – aggression trap since it has not adequately tackled the issues of environmental degradation and large scale corruption in governance of the programme itself. These weaknesses of the programme can be seen as sources of frustration and social entrapment of the Niger Delta that logically can lead to recurrence of violence in the region. Thus, 'although the amnesty program has restored peace as evidenced by the cessation of attacks on oil installations and kidnapping of oil company personnel, violence will most likely reoccur if the frustration – aggression is not addressed' (Ibaba, 2011: 241).

Also, the amnesty program in the Niger Delta has been further criticized for not keeping to the fundamentals of a typical DDR programme either in its conception or operations (see, Ikelegbe, 2006; Davidheiser and Nyiayaana, 2010). Therefore, in relation to the Nigerian case that,

A DDR program is typically adopted as a means of transition from conflict to peace since its function is to remove one or more of the disputing parties from the scene…a DDR program is only expected to comprise the preliminary phases of a much broader process of addressing root causes that initially motivated the combatants. By failing to include the latter, the Amnesty Program does not conform to this model (Davidheiser and Nyiayaana, 2010: 1).

Perhaps, the current emergence of a new militant group known as the Niger Delta Avengers (NDA) in 2016 bears eloquent testimony to the deficiencies of the programme to tackle the problems in the Niger Delta in either sustainable or effective manner.

In spite of the worries about the plague of resource curse in Nigeria and the knowledge sponsored jinx of unsustainable development in oil economies, there is no doubt that resource endowment is a positive attribute for any state in Africa as elsewhere. Therefore, what matters essentially is the way and manner or process of oil exploitation and resource management. Basically the case of Norway which has done very well with its North Sea oil endowment should be a beacon of hope that there is nothing inherently evil in oil resource endowment. Therefore, oil endowment can become good when as Afeikhena (2005) argues, the revenues from it are managed transparently, accountably and fairly. It is only on these principles that such resources would be made to generate the good of the greater number and enhance genuine development in these nations.

There is no doubting the fact that the discussion of the occult along the lines I have pursued in this book may be seen as privileging the notion of Africa as still the backwaters of the world and where anything is literally possible. This thinking should be considered largely untenable and tantamount to a blunt refusal to appreciate inclusive knowledge and worldviews especially when such does not meet the assumed dispassionate objectivity of Western science. Be that as it may, I have also tried to make the case that occult practices are not peculiar to Africa;

they are rather global phenomena which take various shapes and shades in various societies. In spite of the most nationalistic or patriotic of intentions, to argue that occult is a thing of the past or that it is a narrative of the traditional past or the rural backward enclaves in Africa is to engage in denial or obtuse refusal to negotiate reality. Without doubt the invocation of the *Egbesu* deity and its role or utility in the Niger Delta conflict often draws ambiguous responses even from those who ideally ought to know. The *Egbesu* in this case literally resembles the classical, 'I can't put my fingers on it', which implies that though I feel or sense it I cannot make a concrete connection or contact. Therefore, the phenomenon is usually reported in the following manner:

> Indeed, there are allegations that members of Egbesu swear oaths of allegiance to the Egbesu deity, and undergo certain rituals, which fortify them against bullets and assure them of victory in battle. This has been used to explain the daring and precision with which the Egbesu militants have launched some of their attacks, and co-ordinated the struggle in the delta (Obi, 2001: 72).

In spite of the above, those who have made contact with the militants in the late 2000s like Junger (2007), Ghazvinian (2007) and my own field experience would agree with the following largely incontrovertible facts:

I.   A generalized subscription to the *Egbesu* deity by MEND and other Ijaw militant groups in the conflict

II.   Scarifications on the bodies of the militants deemed as fortification against enemies

III. Extensive use of amulets and charms by these militants

IV.   Militant camps where entry for visitors is regulated by rituals and the prominence of shrines in some of them

V.   A tendency among the youth militants to allude to the powers of *Egbesu* as the source of their strength and a belief that

179

the violence is justified in the sight of the deity since it is an attempt to liberate the Ijaw from servitude and domestic colonialism.

In spite of the above, my own investigation in addition established the shift in deployment and reinvention of the *Egbesu* deity occasioned by the conflict. This exists mainly on two grounds. In the first case, the *Egbesu* deity just like other deities in many communities in Africa suffered the negative impact of the colonial intervention which heralded the coming of western education and the world religions which as the years went by made deities like *Egbesu* to decline in both importance and relevance to the people who have found new ways of life and a stronger belief system. Therefore, the *Egbesu* was heading for certain extinction before it was re-invented in some sense by the Ijaw youth militants who found a good use for it in the conflict.

Secondly, and related to the above is that the re-invention of the deity necessitated some changes or modification of what the deity represented. Hence, while the imaginations of the youth militants I spoke to captured *Egbesu* as the god of war and the armada of all struggles of the Ijaw against oppression; the older Ijaws I spoke with see the *Egbesu* more or less in its ideal state as symbolizing truth, justice and liberation. Thus, while they did not describe *Egebsu* as a god of war in order to avoid associating it with violence, they all the same saw it as privileging liberation and that its use by youth along this line is in order.

In addition to the above, the deployment of the deity to the war effort has equally bred the extension of the perceived purposes of the deity in the imaginations of the Ijaw youth militants. In this sense, the *Egbesu* deity determines which war is justified (which incidentally to my respondents meant all the actions of the militants); the deity also plays a role in determining the weapons to be utilized for the war; and the role of the high priest and messengers of the deity who are generally seen as the human agents that mediate these various roles of the deity.

Another thing clearly borne out by the study is that in comparing the use of the *Egbesu* deity by the youth in the Niger Delta with similar incidences elsewhere in the African continent like the cases in the Congo, Sierra Leone or Liberia for that matter, I can see a fundamental and instructive difference in the notion of cultural inversion and cultural revision. In this case, while the situation in these other places involved more or less the utilization of the occult or witchcraft in the process of cultural inversion by young people, in the Niger Delta it was simply a case of waking up an almost redundant cultural agency.

Therefore, re-inventing the occult helped the young people transform roles or achieve role reversals and blunt the likely guilty complex of atrocities committed during the war (see, Jourdan 2004; Beneduce et al, 2006) in these other zones of conflict. But in the case of the youth in the Niger Delta region of Nigeria, the invocation of the *Egbesu* deity resembles a type of cultural revision in which the young people re-imagined what exited in the traditional culture of the Ijaw and imbued this element of traditional religious belief and practice with new role as a critical repository of agency of change in the turbulent Niger delta environment.

But even more interesting is that the use of the *Egbesu* deity by Ijaw youth militants while implicating a cultural revision is also symptomatic of the need to deal with and modify the structure of opportunities and access to economic resources offered by the Nigerian state. In this sense, the *Egbesu* deity can be perceived as popular among Ijaw youth militants and in this sense it has become a rallying point in the conflict (see, Gore and Pratten, 2003: 233):

The foregoing observations offer a fundamental plank of difference between the *Egbesu* phenomenon and the utilization of the occult or magic in other conflict zones in Africa. Hence, while such nihilistic and arcane acts of magic like the eating of dead enemies by some units of the Kamajor militias in Sierra Leone (see Alie, 2005); the inversion of culture and cultural roles

181

entailed in fighting while dressed as women in the case of the Liberia youth militias (see, Ellis, 1999); and the bizarre rituals of youth militias in Kivu DR. Congo (see, Jourdan, 2004) all point to a general deployment of terror, numbing of conscience in the wake of violence, and a product of the tensions and anxieties of role inversion among the youth engaged in conflict, the *Egbesu* deity in the Niger Delta case goes beyond the general and common manifestations of such practices.

Therefore, the use of the deity in the Niger Delta by the militants does not just entail the deployment of an ancient reliable deity to war but rather serves more crucially as a rallying point of cultural solidarity and the imaginations of an ideal society and environment devoid of socio-economic marginalization, environmental degradation, exploitation, disempowerment and other perceived evils of the capitalist state regulated oil exploitation regime in the region. The occult in this instance clearly approximates a symbolic and spiritual embodiment of the desires and fantasies of liberation by the youth militants. Without doubt, the revival or revision of such a cultural phenomenon in the context of violence and bloodletting signals an orgiastic desire for a pre-colonial past where resources and their ownership and exploitation are privileged through local idioms and social practices reflective of a Pan-Ijaw frame of social relations.

Ideally, anthropologists and other scholars of society expected that the project of modernity would lead to the extinction of occult practices and beliefs (see for instance, Pile, 2006; Marwick, 1975). This expectation arose mainly from the perception of witchcraft and occult as only viable among close-knit and intimate kin and family groups where there was little chance of expressing deep hatred which threatened the whole group and where banding together and solidarity were imperative tools in dealing with external aggression. In this case, social norms forbade expressing such deep resentments or grievances with other family members and those who feel thus aggrieved and not satisfied with the mechanism of resolving difference in the family and kin group easily took the secret alternative to getting redress and this meant invoking the occult. In such a situation the use of supernatural means to inflict harm on enemies or express hatred became popular. Therefore, the emergence of modernity and growth of urbanization would break these traditional family and kin groups as main units of habitation and usher in diverse groups made up of people from heterogeneous social backgrounds who in the former traditional setting would have been strangers to each other.

As a result, Marwick (1975: 380) contends that, 'in the towns, a preponderance of strangers not linked intimately or emotionally makes it possible for hostility to be expressed openly rather than supernaturally'. In fact, the above sentiments find company in the earlier views of a popular member of the famed Chicago School of Sociology, Robert Park who argued consistently that magic or occult can only survive outside the realm of the modern city (see, Park 1925/1984). In this sense, science and city cultures represent higher stages of cultural development than magic and folk cultures.

In spite of the fact that the above picture of occult emerged over a misconception of the nature and manifestation of the occult especially its nature as a cultural element bound with cultural and existential experiences of people around the world, the optimism of people like Marwick has also been rendered impotent and void by the incapacity of the modern state especially in Africa and the growing resentment which the injustice in the modern state project in most of Africa has generated especially among those who are far from the corridors of power and privilege. As Abbink (2014) succinctly captures it, religion now seems the alternative discourse of empowerment in these African societies i.e. people are now increasingly empowered via their religious affiliation rather than through politics. But the above nexus between modernity and occult is not by any means peculiarly African since authors like Pile (2006) contends that the modern city did not simply kill off magic instead magical practices and techniques are part and parcel of the very stuff of the modern experience.

Despite the fact that the reverse would likely be the situation in Europe (at least, on the surface), what the *Egbesu* case eloquently shows and what can be said to be the case across many African contemporary societies is that modernization or the rationalization of life does not globally lessen the influence of religion. As a matter of fact, there are glaring evidences[69] of even modernity especially through the new media heightening and intensifying both the presence and influence of religion in African societies rather than making societies lose or neglect their religious faith.

---

[69] Witness the rapid growth and immense proselytization especially from the Pentecostal churches in many African nations – Nigeria, Ghana and South Africa are ready examples. There is also the heavy deployment of new media technologies into the arena of worship through acoustic channels; televangelism; video; social media etc. which have seriously narrowed and often obviated the distinction between religious space and public space

References

Abbink, Jon (2014). "Religion and Politics in Africa: The Future of "The Secular". *Africa Spectrum,* Vol. 49; No. 3: 83 - 106

Adebayo, A.G (1993). *Embattled Federalism: history of revenue allocation in Nigeria, 1946 – 1990.* New York: Peter Lang

Adedeji, A (1999). "Cleansing the Augean Stables". *Africa Today, Vol. 5 (May): 32*

Afeikhena, J (2005). "Managing Oil Rent for Sustainable Development and Poverty Reduction in Africa". Paper presented at the UNU-WIDER Conference on "Thinking Ahead: The Future of Development Economics". http: //62.237.131.23/conference/conference-2005-3/conference-2005-3-papers/Jerome.pdf   Accessed: 14 October 2009

Aghedo, Iro (2014). "Old Wine in a New Wine Bottle: Ideological and Operational Linkages between Maitatsine and Boko Haram Revolts in Nigeria". *African Security,* 7: 229 - 250

Aimaize, E and Sam Oyadongha (2005). "FG Deploys Soldiers, Gunboats in Bayelsa". Legal Oil. http://www.legaloil.com/NewsItem.asp?DocumentIDX= 1135808654&Category=news Accessed: 28 April 2007

Alagoa, E.J (1999). "Peoples of the Cross River Valley and the Eastern Niger Delta", in O. Ikime (ed.) *Groundwork of Nigerian History.* Ibadan: Heinemann Educational Books, pp. 56 - 72

Alagoa, E.J (1972). *A History of the Niger Delta.* Ibadan: Heinemann Educational Books

Alagoa, E.J (1970). "Long - Distance Trade and States in the Niger Delta". *Journal of African History,* Vol. 11; No. 3: 319 - 329

Alagoa, E. J and A. Fombo (1972). *A Chronicle of Grand Bonny.* Ibadan: Heinemann

185

Alausa, Wale (2009). "Otuba Gbenga Daniel is Treacherous – Text of Press Conference by Wale Alausa". Sahara Reporters, http://www.saharareporters.com/index.php?option=com_content&view=article&id=3139Accessed: 14th October 2009

Allen, Chris (1995). "Understanding African Politics". *Review of African Political Economy*, 22; No. 65: 301 - 320

Allie, Joe (2005). "The Kamajor Militia in Sierra Leone: Liberators or Nihilists", in David Francis (ed.) *Civil Militia: Africa's Intractable Security Menace*. Aldershot England: Ashgate Pub. Pp; 51 – 70

Anugwom, E.E (2014). "Beyond Oil: Environmental Rights, Travel, Local Knowledge and Youth Conflict in the Oil-Rich Niger Delta of Nigeria". *Africa Today*, Vol. 61 (2): 21 – 39

Anugwom, E.E (2010). "The Bonnke Effect: Encounters with Transnational Evangelism in Southeastern Nigeria", in Afe Adogame and Jim Pickard (eds) *Religion Crossing Boundaries: Transnational Religious and Social Dynamics in Africa and the New Africa Diaspora*. Leiden: Brill Pub. Pp. 211 - 226

Anugwom, E.E (2009). "Women, Education and Work in Nigeria". *Educational Research and Reviews, 4 (4): 127 - 134*

Anugwom, E.E (2008). "Contested Terrain: Economic Migration, Islamic Sharia Law and Ethno-Religious Conflict in Nigeria". *African Study Monographs, 29 (4): 159 - 181*

Anugwom, E.E (2007). "Stuck in the Middle: Women, ICTs and the Struggle for Survival in the Oil Degraded Niger Delta Environment, Nigeria". *AGENDA, Issue 72: 58 - 68*

Anugwom, E.E (2005). "Oil Minorities and Politics of Resource Control in Nigeria". *Africa Development*, Vol. xxx; No. 4: 87 - 120

Anugwom, E.E (2004). "Ethnicity, Federalism and Revenue Allocation in a Democratic Nigeria: the Niger Delta Problem". *Africa Insight, Vol. 34; No.2/3: 23 – 30*

Anugwom, E. (2001). 'The Military, Ethnicity and Democracy in Nigeria', *Journal of Social Development in Africa*, Vol. 16, No. 2: 93-114.

Anugwom, E.E (2000). "Ethnic Conflict and Democracy in Nigeria: The Marginalization Question". *Journal of Social Development in Africa, Vol. 15, No. 1*

Ashforth, Adam (2005). *Witchcraft, Violence and Democracy in South Africa.* Chicago: University of Chicago Press.

Auty, R (1993). *Sustaining Development in Mineral Economies: the resource curse thesis.* London: Routledge

Auty, R.M and A. Warhurst (1991). "Sustainable Development in Mineral-Driven Economies". Working Paper, University of Lancaster

Azaiki S (2003). *Inequities in Nigeria Polities: The Nige-Delta, Resource Control, Underdevelopment and Youth restiveness.* Yenegoa: Treasure communication Resource Ltd.

Bassey, Nnimo (2006). "Trade and Human Rights in the Niger Delta of Nigeria". Pambazuka News, June 1, 2006. http: //www.pambazuka.org/cn/category/comment/34801 Accessed: July 5 2007

Bayart, Jean-Francois, S. Ellis and B. Hibou (1999). *The Criminalization of the State in Africa.* Oxford: James Currey Pub.

Beneduce, R; L. Jourdan; T. Raeymaekers; and K. Vlassenroot (2006). "Violence with a Purpose: Exploring the Functions and Meaning of Violence in the Democratic Republic of Congo". *Intervention*, Vol. 4 No. 1: 32 – 46

Best, S.G and D. von Kemedi (2005). "Armed Groups and Conflict in Rivers and Plateau States, Nigeria", in N. Florquin and Eric Berman (eds) *Armed and Aimless: Armed Groups, Guns, and Human Security in the ECOWAS Region.* Geneva: Small Arms Survey. Pp; 13 - 42

Bilgin, P and A. David (2002). "Historicizing Representations of 'Failed States': Beyond the Cold-War Annexation of the Social Sciences? *Third World Quarterly*, Vol.23, No.1: 55 - 80

187

Binsbergen, Wim (1991). "Becoming a Sangoma: Religious Anthropological Fieldwork in Francistown, Botswana". *Journal of Religion in Africa*, xxi, 4: 309 -343

Boas, M (2001). "Liberia and Sieerra Leone: Dead Ringers? The Logic of Neopatrimonial Rule". *Third World Quarterly*, Vol. 22, Issue 5: 697 – 723

Boyer, Paschal (2001). *Religion Explained: The Human Instincts that Fashion Gods, Spirits and Ancestors.* London: William Heinemann

Bratton, Michael and Nicholas van de Walle (1994). "Neopatrimonial Regimes and Political Transition in Africa". *World Politics*, Vol.46 (4): 453 - 489

Centre for Development and conflict Management Studies (CDCMS) (2003). *Ethnic Militias and the Future of Democracy in Nigeria.* Ile-Ife: Obafemi Awolowo University Press and Heinrich Boll Foundation; http://www.bollnigeria.org/documents/Ethnic20militias.p df Accessed: 28 April 2007

Centre for Development and Democracy (CDD) (2007). *CDD Niger Delta Report.* www.cdd.org.uk/projects/nigeriadelta/nigerdeltaproject3.h tml Accessed: 18 June 2010

Chabal, P and Jean-Paul Daloz (1999). *Africa Works: The Political Instrumentalization of Disorder.* Oxford: James Currey

Collier, Paul (2000). "Doing Well Out of War: An Economic Perspective", in M. Berdal and D. Malone (eds) *Greed and Grievance: Economic Agendas in Civil Wars.* London and Boulder: Lynne Rienner

Collier, P and A. Hoeffler (2001). *Greed and Grievance in Civil War.* World Bank Policy Research Working Paper No. 2355, Washington, D.C: World Bank

Comaroff, J and J. Comaroff (2003). "Transparent Fictions, or the Conspiracies of a Liberal Imagination – An Afterword", in H. West and T. Sanders (eds) *Transparency and Conspiracy:*

Ethnographies of Suspicion in the New World Order. Durham, NC: Duke University Press; Pp; 287 - 300

Comaroff, Jean and John Comaroff (1999). "Occult Economies and the Violence of Abstraction: notes from the South African postcolony". *American Ethnologist,* Vol.26 No. 2 (May): 279 – 303

Comolli, Virginia (2015). *Boko Haram: Nigeria's Islamist Insurgency.* London: C.Hurst and Co

Corden, M and J.P Neary (1982). "Booming Sector and Dutch Disease Economics: a survey". *Economic Journal* 92: 826 – 44

Crick, M (1979). "Anthropologists' Witchcraft: Symbolically Defined or Analytically Undone". *Journal of the Anthropological Society of Oxford,* 10: 139 - 146

Daily Independent (2009). "MEND's Attack on Atlas Cove Jetty"; 16 July (Editorial)

Daily Trust (2009). "Niger Delta Governors have Failed – Activist". October 11 (Sunday).
http://www.news.dailytrust.com/index.php?option=com_content&view=article&id=7 Accessed: 12 October 2009

Danish Immigration Service (2005). Report on Human Rights Issues in Nigeria: Joint British-Danish Fact-Finding Mission to Abuja and Lagos, Nigeria. Copenhagen: The Danish Immigration Service

Davidheiser, M and K. Naiyaana (2010). "Demobilization or Remobilization? The Amnesty Program and Resource, Security and development in the Niger Delta; Yenagoa, Bayelsa State (March 8 – 11)

De Boeck, F .1999. Domesticating Diamonds and Dollars: Identity, Expenditures and Sharing in Southwestern Zaire (1984 – 1997). In *Globalization and Identity: Dialectics of Flow and Closure,* eds. B. Meyer and P. Geschiere, 177 - 209. Oxford: Blackwell

Dessel, J.P (1995). *The Environment Situation in the Niger Delta, Nigeria.* Netherlands: Green Peace

Dirk, Kohnert (2003). "Witchcraft and transnational Social Spaces: Witchcraft Violence, Reconciliation and Development in South Africa's transition Process". *Journal of Modern African Studies*, Vol. 41; No.2: 217 – 245

Dirk, Kohnert (2007). "On the Renaissance of African Modes of Thought – The Example of the Belief in Magic and Witchcraft". http: //mpra.ub.uni-muenchen.de/7019 Accessed: 20 November 2009

Durkheim, E (1954). *The Elementary Forms of the Religious Life.* Glencoe, Illinois: Free Press

Eghosa, O; A. Ikelegbe; O. Olarinmoye; S. Okhonmina (2007). Youth Militias, Self Determination and Resource Control Struggles in the Niger-Delta Region of Nigeria. http: //www.ascleiden.nl/pdf/cdpnigeriaRevisedOsaghae(1)2.p df Accessed: 16 November 2009

Elbadawi, I and N. Sambani (2002). "How much War will We See? Estimating the Prevalence of Civil War in 161 Countries, 1960 – 1999". *Journal of Conflict Resolution* 46, No. 2 (June): 307 - 334

Ellis, Stephen (1999). *The Mask of Anarchy: The Destruction of Liberia and the Religious Dimension to an African Civil War.* London: Hurst and Co.

Environmental Impact Assessment (EIA) (2003). *Women, Environmental Impact Assessment (EIA) and Conflict Issues in the Niger Delta: A Case Study of Gbaran Oil Field Community in Bayelsa State.* Port Harcourt: Earth Rights Institute

Environmental Rights Action/Friends of the Earth Nigeria (ERA/FoEN) (2005). *The Shell Report: Continuing the Abuses in Nigeria 10 years after Ken Saro-Wiwa.* Benin City: ERA/FoEN

Erdman, G and U. Engels (2006). *Neopatrimonialism Revisited – Beyond a Catch-All Concept,* Legitimacy and Efficiency of Political Systems. GIGA Woking Paper. www.giga-hamburg.de/workingpapers Accessed: 20 April 2010

Evans-Pritchard, E.E (1954). *The Institutions of Primitive Society.* Oxford: Blackwell

Francis, D.J (ed.)(2005). *Civil Militia: Africa's Intractable Security Menace?* Aldershot England: Ashgate Pub

Gelb, A.H (1988). *Oil Windfalls: Blessing or Curse?* New York: Oxford University Press

Geschiere, Peter (1997). *The Modernity of Witchcraft: Politics and the Occult in Postcolonial Africa.* Charlottesville and London: University of Virginia Press

Ghazvinian, John (2007). "The Curse of Oil". *Virginia Quarterly Review,* Winter, Vol. 83

Gifford, P (1987). "Africa Shall be Saved". An Appraisal of Reinhard Bonnke's Pan-African Crusade". *Journal of Religion in Africa,* 17 (1): 63 - 92

Gore, C and D. Pratten (2003). "The Politics of Plunder: The Rhetoric of Order and Disorder in Southern Nigeria". *African Affairs,* No. 102: 211 – 240

Goswami, H and R. Kashyap (2006). Tobacco in Movies and Impact on Youth. A Study by Burning Brain Society, India; WHO and Ministry of Health and Family Welfare, India http://smokefreemovies.ucsf.edu/pdf/BurningBrain-tobaccoinmovies.pdf Accessed: 15 October 2009

Grugel, J (2002). *Democratization: A Critical Introduction.* Basingstoke: Palgrave

Harnischfeger, J (2006). "State Decline and the Return of Occult Powers: the case of Prophet Eddy in Nigeria". *Magic, Ritual and Witchcraft* (Summer): 56 - 78

Harrison, P (1982). *Inside the Third World.* London: Paladin Grafton Books

Heller, Patrick (2010). The Nigerian Petroleum Industry Bill: Key Upstream Questions for the National Assembly. http://www.revenuewatch.org/files/RWI_Nigeria_PIB_Analysis.pdf Accessed: 11th May 2011

Hengehold, Laura (2009). Witchcraft, Subjectivation and Sovereignty: Foucault in Cameroon. http://www.sens-public.org/spip.php?article-686 Accessed: 13th October 2009

191

Homer-Dixon, Thomas (1999). *Environment Scarcity and Violence.* Princeton: Princeton University Press

Homer-Dixon, Thomas (1995). "The Ingenuity Gap: Can Poor Countries Adapt to Resource Scarcity?" *Population and Development Review*, 21 No. 3: 587 – 612

Human Rights Watch (1999). The Destruction of Odi and Rape in Choba. http: //www.hrw.org/press/dec/nibg1299.htm Accessed: 5th September 2006

Hutchful, Eboe and K. Aning (2004). "The Political Economy of Conflict", in Adekeye, Adebajo and Ismail Rashid (eds) *West Africa's Security Challenges: building Peace in a troubled Region.* Boulder and London: Lynne Rienner

Ibaba, Samuel (2011). "Amnesty and Peace – Building in the Niger Delta: Addressing the Frustration-Aggression Trap". *Africana*, Vol.5, No.1: 238 – 271

Ifeka, C (2006). "Youth Cultures and the Fetishization of Violence in Nigeria". *Review of African Political Economy*, No. 110: 721 – 736

Ifeka, C. (2000). 'Conflict, Complicity and Confusion: Unravelling empowerment struggles in Nigeria after the return to democracy'. *Review of African Political Economy*, No. 83.

Ikein, A.A and C. Briggs-Anigboh (1998). *Oil and Fiscal Federalism in Nigeria: The Political Economy of Resource Allocation in a Developing Country.* Aldershot: Ashgate

Ikelegbe, A (2006) "Beyond the Threshold of Civil Struggle: Youth Militancy and The Militiazation of the Resource Conflicts in the Niger-delta Region of Nigeria", *African Studies Monographs*, 27(3): 87-122, October.

Ikelegbe, Augustine (2005). "The Economy of Conflict in the Oil Rich Niger Delta Region of Nigeria. *Nordic Journal of African Studies*, Vol. 14 (2): 208 – 234

Ikime, Obaro (1999). "The Peoples and Kingdoms of the Delta Province", in O. Ikime (ed.) *Groundwork of Nigerian History.* Ibadan: Heinemann Educational Books, pp. 89 - 108

Immigration and Refugee Board of Canada (IRB) (2006). Nigeria: Egbesu Boys; Leadership, Membership Recruitment Practices, Activities, and Treatment by Authorities. http://www.unhcr.org/refworld/docid/45f1478a20.html Accessed: 22 October 2009

IRINnews (2007). "Nigeria: Sharp Rise in Hostage Taking may be linked to upcoming elections". http://irinnews.org ; Accessed: 21-09-09

Iyioha, M.A (2008). Leadership, Policy Making and Economic Growth in African Countries: The Case of Nigeria. Working Paper No. 17; Washington D.C: The World Bank/Commission on Growth and Development

Iyioha, M.A and D.E Oriakhi (2008). "Explaining African Economic Growth Performance: The Case of Nigeria", in Benno Ndulu; S.O'Connell; J. Azam; R. Bates; A. Fosu; J. Gunning; and D. Njinkeu (eds). The Political Economy of Economic Growth in Africa, 1960 – 2000, Vol. 2, Country Case Studies. Cambridge: Cambridge University Press

Jenkins, P and D. Maier-Katkin (1992). "Satanism: Myth and Reality in a Contemporary Moral Panic". *Crime, Law and Social Change*; 17 (1): 53 – 75

Joseph, Richard A. (1987). *Democracy and Prebendal Politics in Nigeria: The Rise and Fall of the Second Republic.* London: Cambridge University Press

Jourdan, Luca (2004). "Being at War, Being Young: Violence and Youth in Northern Kivu", in K. Vlassenroot and T. Raeymaekers (eds) *Conflict and Social Transformation in Eastern Dr. Congo.* Gent: Academia Press. Pp.; 157 – 176

Junger, S (2007). "Crude Awakening, Part Two". The Observer Online, http://observer.guardian.co.uk/magazine/story/0,,205544 23,00html Accessed: 16 April 2007

Keen, David (2000). "Incentives and Disincentives for Violence", in M. Berdal and D. Malone (eds) op. cit.

193

Kemedi, Dimieari (2006). *Fuelling the Violence: Non-State Armed Actors in the Niger Delta. Economies of Violence* Working Paper No.10; Berkeley, California: Institute of International Studies

Krugman, P.R (1987). "The Narrow Band, the Dutch Disease and the Competitive Consequences of Mrs Thatcher". *Journal of Development Economics* 27: 41 - 55

Lazzarei, Thomas (2016). "Ogoniland Oil Spills clean up will take up to 30 years". Africa Europe Faith and Justice Network (AEFJN). https://www.aefjn.org/index.php/370/articles/ogoniland-oil-spills-clean-up-will-take-up-to-30-years.html Accessed: 21 September 2016

Leib, Arthur (1946). "The Mystical Significance of Colours". *Folklore* 57: 128 – 133

Loimeier, Roman (2012). "Boko Haram: The Development of a Militant Religious Movemennt in Nigeria". *Africa Spectrum*, 47 (2-3): 137 – 155

Lubeck, P; Watt, M & Lipschutz, R (2007). *Convergent Interests: U.S. Energy Security and the "Securing" of Nigerian Democracy.* International Policy Report (February), Centre for International Policy, Washington, D.C

Marwick, Max (1975).*Witchcraft and Sorcery: Selected Readings.* Harmondsworth: Penguin

Mbanefo, Gini (1993). "Unsettled Issues in Nigerian Fiscal Federalism and the National Question", in F.Onah (ed.) *The National Question and Economic Development in Nigeria.* Ibadan: Nigerian Economic Society

Mbebe, A (2002). "African Modes of Self-Writing". *Public Culture,* 14 (1): 239 -273

Moore, H and T. Sanders (eds) (2001). *Magical Interpretations, Material Realities: modernity, witchcraft and the occult in Postcolonial Africa.* London: Routledge

Naanen, Ben (1995). "Oil-Producing Minorities and the Restructuring of Nigerian Federalism: the case of the Ogoni people". *Journal of Commonwealth and Comparative Politics, 33, 1:* 46-78

Nankani, G (1979). "Development Problems of Mineral Exporting Countries". World Bank Staff Working Paper 354, Washington D.C: World Bank

Nigeria National Petroleum Corporation (NNPC) (2010). The Petroleum Industry Bill. http: //www.nnpcgroup.com/PublicRelations/PetroleumIndust ryBill.aspx Accessed: 11th May 2011

Nolutshungu, S (1996) (ed.) *Margins of Insecurity: minorities and international security.* New York: University of Rochester Press

Nyamnjoh, Francis (2005). "Images of Nyongo amongst Bamenda Grassfielders in Whiteman Kontri". *Citizenship Studies,* 9 (3): 241-269.

Obi, Cyril (2008).Nigeria's Niger Delta: understanding the complex drivers of conflict. FOI Lecture Series on African Security; Nordiska Afrikainstitutet

Obi, Cyril (2007). "The Struggle for Resource Control in a Petro-State: a perspective from Nigeria", in P. Bowles; H. Veltmeyer; S. Cornilissen; N. Invernizzi; T. Kwong-leung (eds) *National Perspectives on Globalisation.* New York and Hampshire: Palgrave Macmillan

Obi, Cyril (2006). *Youth and the Generational Dimensions to Struggles for Resource Control in the Niger Delta: Prospects for the Nation – State Project in Nigeria.* CODESRIA Monograph Series, Dakar: CODESRIA

Obi, Cyril (2001). The Changing Forms of Identity Politics in Nigeria under Economic Adjustment: The Case of the Oil Minorities Movement of the Niger Delta. Research Report No.119; Uppsala: Nordiska Afrikainstitutet

Obi, C.I (1999). *The Crisis of Environmental Governance in the Niger Delta 1985 – 1996.* Occasional Paper Series 3/3. Harare: African Political Science Association

Okafo, Nonso (2005). "Foundations of Okija Justice".

http://nigeriaworld.com/articles/2005/mar/033.html
Accessed: 23 November 2009

Okhomina, Osamede (2010). The Nigerian Petroleum Industry
Bill (PIB). Energy Global,
http://www.energyglobal.com/sectors/processing/articles
/The_Nigerian_Petroleum_Industry_Bill.aspx   Accessed:
11th May 2011

Okilo, Melford (1980). "The Derivation Principle and National
Unity". *Daily Times* (July 9): 4

Okonta, I (2008). *When Citizens Revolt: Nigerian elites, big oil and the
Ogoni struggle for self-determination.* Trenton, New Jersey and
Asmara: Africa World Press

Okonta, Ike (2006). Behind the Mask: Explaining the
Emergence of the MEND Militia in Nigeria's Oil-Bearing
Niger Delta. Economies of Violence Working Paper No.11;
Berkeley, California: Institute of International Studies

Okonta, I and O. Doughlas (2001). *Where Vultures Feast – Shell,
Human Rights, and Oil in the Niger Delta.* New York: Sierra
Club Books

Onwuemedo, S (2000). "We will not give up this Fight – Niger
Delta Leaders". *Weekend Vanguard (Jan.)*

Omeje, K (2006). *High Stakes and Stakeholders: oil conflict and security
in Nigeria.* Aldershot, Hampshire: Ashgate Pub.

Omeje, K (2005a). "The Egbesu and Bakassi Boys: African
Spiritism and the Mystical Re-traditionalisation of Security",
in David Francis (ed.) *Civil Militia: Africa's Intractable Security
Menace?* Aldershot England: Ashgate Pub. Pp; 71 -88

Omeje, K (2005b). "Oil Conflict in Nigeria: Contending Issues
and Perspectives of the Local Niger Delta People". *New
Political Economy, Vol. 10; No. 3*

Omeje, K. (2004), 'The State, Conflict and Evolving Politics in
the Niger Delta Nigeria.' *Review of African Political Economy.*
101. 425-440.

Ordinioha, Best and Brisibe, Seiyefa (2013). "The Health
Implications of Crude Oil Spills in the Niger Delta, Nigeria:

An Interpretation of Published Studies". *Nigeria Medical Journal*, 54 (1): 10 - 16

Oruwari, Yomi (2006). Post – Conflict Peace Building and Democracy in an Oil Region: The Role of Women's Groups in the Niger Delta Region, Nigeria. Berkeley California: Institute of International Studies

Oruwari, Y and O. Owei .2006. Youth in Urban Violence in Nigeria: A Case Study of Urban Gangs from Port Harcourt. Our Niger Delta Project, Port Harcourt Nigeria

Owen, A (2004). *The Place of Enchantment: British Occultism and the Culture of the Modern*. Chicago IL: University of Chicago Press

Owen, A (1989). *The Darkened Room: Women, Power and Spiritualism in Late Victorian England*. Chicago IL: University of Chicago Press

Park, R.E (1925/1984). "Magic, Mentality and City Life", in R. Parks; and E. Burgess with R. Mckenzie and L. Wirth (eds) *The City: Suggestions for Investigation of Human Hehavior in the Urban Environment*. Chicago, IL: University of Chicago Press; Pp. 80 – 98

Phil-Eze, P.O (2001). "Biodiversity and Environmental Problems in Nigeria", in G.E.K Ofomata and P.O Phil-Eze (eds) *Geographical Perspectives on Environmental Problems and Management in Nigeria*, pp. 33 – 52

Phil-Eze and I.C Okoro (2009). "Sustainable Biodiversity Conservation in the Niger Delta: A Practical Approach to Conservation Site Selection". *Biodiversity and Conservation*, 18 (5): 1247 - 1257

Pile, Steve (2006). "The Strange Case of Western Cities: Occult Globalisations and the Making of Urban Modernity". *Urban Studies*, Vol. 43, No. 2: 305 - 318

Ranger, Terence (2007). "Scotland Yard in the Bush: medicine murders, child witches and the construction of the occult: a literature review". Africa 77 (2): 272 – 283

Ross, Michael (2003). "Oil, Drugs and Diamonds: the varying roles of natural resources in civil war", in Karen Ballentine and Jake Sherman (eds) *The Political Economy of Armed Conflict: Beyond Greed and Grievance*. Colorado and London: Lynne Rienner. Pp; 47 – 70

Sachs, J.D and A.M Warner (2001). "The Curse of National Resources". *European Economic Review, 45: 827-838*

Sachs, J.D and A.M Warner (1995). "National Resources Abundance and Economic Growth". No. 517a. Cambridge, MA: Harvard Institute for International Development *Development Discussion Paper*

Saro-Wiwa, K (1995). *A Month and A Day: A Detention Diary*. London: Penguin Books

Saro-Wiwa, Ken (1994). Ogoni: Moment of Truth. Port Harcourt: Saros International

Saro-Wiwa, Ken (1992). *Genocide in Nigeria: The Ogoni Tragedy*. Port Harcourt: Saros International

Schmidt, Steffen W; James C. Scott; Carl Lande and Laura Guasti (1977) (eds). *Friends, Followers and Factions*. New Jersey: Prentice Hall

Snow, Donald (1996). *Uncivil Wars*. Boulder: Lynee Rienner

South African Pagan Rights Alliance (SAPRA) (2009). Press Releases.   http://www.paganrightsalliance.org/press.html Accessed: 14th October 2009

Spiro, Melford (1969). "Religion: Problems of Definition and Explanation", in M. Banton (ed.) *Anthropological Approaches to the Study of Religion*. London: Tavistock pp.85 – 126

de Soysa, I (2000). "The Resource Curse: Are Civil Wars Driven by Rapacity or Paucity", in M. Berdal and D. Malone (eds) *Greed and Grievance: Economic Agendas in Civil Wars*. Boulder and London: Lynne Rienner

Standefer, R (1979). "The Symbolic Attributes of the Witch". *Journal of Anthropological Society of Oxford* X: 31 - 47

Stiglitz, Joseph (2004). The Resource Curse Revisited. Project Syndicate.

http://www.projectsyndicate.org/commentaries/comment ary_text.php4?id=1656&lang=1&m=contributor.htm Accessed: 16 April 2009

Suberu, R (2001). *Federalism and Ethnic Conflict in Nigeria.* Washington, D.C: United States Institute of Peace Press

Sugishita, Kaori (2009). "Traditional Medicine, Biomedicine and Christianity in Modern Zambia". Africa, Vol.79; No. 3: 435 - 454

te Haar, Gerrie and S. Ellis (2009). "The Occult Does Not Exist: A Response to Terence Ranger". *Africa*, 79 (3): 399 - 412

Tebbe, Nelson (2007). "Witchcraft and Statecraft: Liberal Democracy in Africa". The Georgetown Law Journal, vol. 96: 183 – 236

The Communication Initiative Network (2003). "Effects of Culture and Environment on the Behaviour of Namibian Youth".   http://www.commint.com/node/213316/36 Accessed: 15 October 2009

Thompson, A (2004). *An Introduction to African Politics.* London: Routledge

Torvik, R (2001). "Learning by Doing and the Dutch Disease". *European Economic Review, 45: 285-306*

Turner, Victor .W (1969). "Colour Classification in Ndembu Ritual", in M. Banton (ed.) *Anthropological Approaches to the Study of Religion.* London: Tavistock pp. 47 – 84

Ude, J (2000). "Petroleum Revenue Management: The Nigerian Perspective". Paper presented at World Bank/IFC Petroleum Revenue Management Workshop, Washington D.C, October 23-24

Ukeje, C (2001). "Youths, Violence and the Collapse of Public Order in the Niger Delta of Nigeria". *Africa Development* xxvi; Nos. 1&2: 337-366

Ujomu, P.O (2002). "Social Conflicts, Resources Distribution and Social Justice in Nigeria". *Journal of Asian and African Studies, No. 63: 197-228*

United Nations Development Programme (UNDP) (2006). *Niger Delta Human Development Report.* Abuja: UNDP Nigeria

United Nations Environmental Programme (UNEP) (2011). Environmental Assessment of Ogoniland. Nairobi: UNEP

Weber, Max (1947). *The Theory of Social and Economic Organization.* Translated by A.M Henderson and Talcott Parsons. London: The Free Press

Wescott, Joan (1961). "The Sculpture and Myths of Eshu-Elegba, the Yoruba Trickster". *Africa* 32 (4)

Wijnbergen, S (1984). "The 'Dutch Disease': a disease after all?" *Economic Journal 94: 41-45*

World Bank (1995). *Defining an Environmental Strategy for the Niger Delta.* Washington DC: World Bank